Sue Knaup is the founder and executive director of One Street, a nonprofit serving bicycle advocacy organizations around the world. She has led organizations for more than forty years in the fields of animal rights, environment, special populations, and bicycle advocacy. Sue also owned and operated a bike shop for thirteen years.

Sue is available for speaking engagements. She specializes in interactive presentations that connect attendees to the materials being presented. Sue's workshops are even more hands on, ensuring that each participant leaves with personalized resources.

Contact her at sue@onestreet.org or visit OneStreet.org.

Also by Sue Knaup:

*Defying Poverty with Bicycles: How to Succeed with
Your Own Social Bike Business Program*

*Cures for Ailing Organizations: Revive Your Organization
and Keep It Healthy*

*Backyard Aluminum Casting: for Bike Shift Levers and
Nearly Anything Else*

BIKE HUNT

A MEMOIR

SUE KNAUP

Copyright © 2017 by Sue Knaup

All rights reserved. No portion of this book may be reproduced for large-scale production, posting to the internet, sales, or distribution, by any process or technique, without the express written permission of the publisher.

Publisher's Cataloging-in-Publication data

Names: Knaup, Sue, author.
Title: Bike hunt : a memoir / by Sue Knaup.
Description: Prescott, AZ : One Street Press, 2017.
Identifiers: ISBN 978-0-9859889-3-7

Subjects: LCSH Knaup, Sue. | Cycling. | Bullying in the workplace. | Leadership--Moral and ethical aspects. | Social entrepreneurship. | Social action. | Social change. | BISAC BIOGRAPHY & AUTOBIOGRAPHY / Personal memoirs | BIOGRAPHY & AUTOBIOGRAPHY / Social Activists

Classification: LCC GV1051.A1 2017 | DDC 796.6--dc23

First Edition

ISBN 978-0-9859889-3-7

One Street Press
P.O. Box 3309
Prescott, Arizona 86302
USA

www.OneStreet.org

Printed in the United States of America

To my mother for showing me how to face abuse with grace and dignity.

CONTENTS

1	*Falling*	11
2	*I'm In*	31
3	*Fear or Trust*	53
4	*Delusions*	81
5	*Bully*	101
6	*Power Gauge*	125
7	*Clinging*	151
8	*Best,*	181
9	*Shattering*	185
10	*This*	207

Acknowledgements   219

1
Falling

Out of breath, I spotted the bike shop from a block away, nestled amongst narrow two and three-story historic brick buildings. Its tall front windows angled inward to create a glass entryway and a hint of the tall ceilings inside. Even as I crossed the street to admire the sunlit row of used bikes out front, their tangled handlebars, bright colors, baskets, and bells, I expected to settle on a backroom beater I could fix myself and save money. Their price tags ranged from just over one hundred to well over two hundred dollars—out of my budget.

I'd run ten blocks through downtown Philadelphia having ditched the end of a session at my first national bicycle advocacy conference. I couldn't sit through another minute talking about bikes without having one to ride. So I'd turned to the bike-shops section of a phonebook and bolted out the door toward the closest one. It was September 2000, three years after I'd founded a local bicycle and pedestrian nonprofit in Prescott, Arizona where I still owned and operated my own bike shop.

My eye stopped on a gem—a petite girls-frame Schwinn cruiser from the '60s, one-speed with pedal-back coaster brake. Her swooping metallic-blue curves sparkled, accented by perfect chrome and pinstriped fenders.

"She's lovely, isn't she."

The voice startled me and I turned to find a middle-aged man, front wrapped with a greasy grey shop apron, standing behind me. We chatted about how well the bike's previous owner had cared for her. When I told him I owned a bike shop, his smudged face beamed. He was the owner of this shop. We shook hands and traded names, shared a bit of shop talk about the autumn push before winter and a few laughs about not being in it for the money.

That reminded me the Schwinn was out of my price range. I stumbled over my explanation that I was looking for a used bike not yet tuned, something cheap to ride for the rest of the week during the conference. I could fix it out on the sidewalk and not get in their way.

"Look," he said with an amused expression, "you want this beauty, not some hunk of junk. I'll tell you what. I'll sell her to you for seventy-five dollars. If you bring her back in the same condition, I'll give you your seventy-five dollars back." I couldn't tell which of us was more pleased with this deal.

I didn't know at the time, but that simple moment of bike camaraderie became the seedling of the Bike Hunt. No matter where I traveled in the world, all I needed was to connect with one kind person who would enjoy helping me find a bike.

I had anticipated a similar camaraderie at a two-day workshop on the New Jersey shore right before the conference. It was the annual retreat for local bike-group leaders like me, offered by the Thunderhead Alliance, a national coalition of these organizations. For two days I learned about implementing initiatives from the other attendees, except for the chair of the Thunderhead board who stayed on the perimeter, watching us. On the first evening, he sprawled his long, lanky body over a plastic lounge chair on the motel patio where we gathered, hands behind his frizzy grey hair, smirking past his beak nose as if he owned us. Even at the conference, I caught him studying advocates, glowering at them and sometimes me. On group bike rides in the evenings I pedaled the little Schwinn away from his glare.

I named the bike Pony, like a trusty mount I could nudge to speed. When I took her back to the bike shop and the owner gave me back my seventy-five dollars, I was sorry to let her go.

Back in Prescott after the Philadelphia conference, I was eager to continue discussions with the leaders of the Thunderhead Alliance. But they either answered my calls or emails with curt single sentences or not at all. This didn't surprise me. For two years prior to their retreat, I'd sent emails and letters to Thunderhead requesting that Prescott Alternative Transportation (PAT), the bicycle and pedestrian nonprofit I'd founded, be accepted as a member organization. They never responded. There was no membership form. For all I knew it was a secret, elite club, by invitation only. Then I'd sent a letter with a check and they'd finally made us a member with a brief email just in time for me to attend their retreat on the New Jersey shore. I assumed this exclusivity was part of the Thunderhead culture and accepted that I'd need to earn their friendship over time.

That winter, I applied tips from Philadelphia to projects in my smaller city of Prescott, working with PAT helpers to reverse the trend of high-speed roads back to a place where neighbors could greet each other in the middle of any street, where any kid could bicycle away. Even as I argued with traffic engineers over bike-lane treatments or proper radii for path corners, I kept an eye out for opportunities to return to the national level of bicycle advocacy where I was sure my efforts could reach many more communities. An opportunity finally appeared in an emailed announcement about the first National Bike Summit in Washington, D.C. in March 2001 to bring bicycle advocates to Capitol Hill to lobby Congress. I immediately registered and began planning my first visit to D.C.

Because the National Bike Summit was focused on lobbying Congress, I looked forward to comparing it with my lobbying experience in Sacramento, California's capital, as an animal rights lobbyist with the Fund for Animals, a national nonprofit. That was one of my early activist jobs, starting at age thirteen. While I was working for the Fund's California chapter, we succeeded in banning the use of the decompression chamber for euthanizing animals and set the stage for banning leg-hold traps and hunting of mountain lions in that state. We also thwarted language in countless unrelated bills that would have allowed cruelty to animals.

My experiences in Sacramento had shown me the immense impact lobbying could bring to a state, so I imagined a chance to lobby in Washington would be fifty times greater. Plus I'd see some of the people I'd met in Philadelphia and hoped we could continue the discussions we had there. I also looked forward to repeating the success of the Philadelphia Bike Hunt. Neither worked out as I'd hoped. Instead, I found a new, unexpected friend and her enchanting bike.

Karen was a campaign director at the Rails-to-Trails Conservancy, a national nonprofit that specializes in turning abandoned railway corridors into public trails. Since they were one of the sponsors of the Summit, Karen had offered to host an out-of-town Summit attendee, and she got me. Later she told me she was sure she'd been stuck with some deranged surfer chick, partly due to my attire. I'd stopped along the way to her office to buy a white baseball cap from a street vendor because it was the closest thing they had to a warm hat that would stave off the March cold and drizzling rain. I stood in her office, the cap on backwards, my long blond braid dripping down my backside, trying to explain that I had to hunt for a used bike before going over to her apartment.

"But I've got a perfectly good spare bike at my apartment you can use," Karen said from behind her paper-strewn desk, backlit by the damp grey city through the wall of windows, her bright smile and cheerful demeanor fading from her small, fit frame, her once welcoming brown eyes narrowing to slits.

"You don't understand," I said. "I like looking for used bikes. I'll get to see Washington as I look for one."

"You don't need to look for a bike. I've got one at my apartment."

"But I could see the city as I look."

Karen sucked in air, her eyes rolling to the ceiling. "You can ride the bike around and see the city. Here's the key to my apartment. Here's the key to the bike lock. The bike is in the basement."

She was clearly ready for me to leave her office and I had run out of ways of explaining my primal need to hunt for a bike, to actually own the bike for the duration of my stay. Without realizing,

I was in the midst of forming what would become one of my Bike Hunt rules: Never limit yourself to places where you think you'll find your bike. In this case, it meant not even limiting myself to the Bike Hunt.

Being a greenhorn bike hunter at the time, my disappointment clouded my mood. Fortunately, Karen couldn't follow me back to her apartment so she didn't have to endure my whining, which I kept under my breath as I sat on the hard subway seat and walked the short trek to her apartment building. As soon as I saw Karen's bike, my pity party ended.

I first caught sight of her from the top of the basement stairs. She was locked to the railing, her swept-back chrome handlebar entangled in the metal rails. Even from there, I knew she was special—a "mixtie" frame from the '60s or '70s when a few artful French frame designers had discovered they could replace the top frame bar with two elegant narrow bars lacing the front of the bike to the rear hub. I descended the stairs, my eyes riveted. Her champagne paint was perfect, her tall narrow wheels were made for speed. Suddenly I was the luckiest gal in D.C. because I could borrow Karen's bike.

I pulled her out from her dark confinement and pedaled the rest of the afternoon discovering D.C.'s diversity as I crossed from neighborhood to neighborhood or coasted along a stream that could have been miles from the city. Karen's apartment was in Adams Morgan, an eclectic neighborhood north of downtown where all the varied personalities of Washington collided. A few pedal strokes farther north I found rundown apartments and parks where people gathered outside. Street vendors sold odd assortments and children played in the streets. To the west, I crossed a bridge over a park laced with trails and onto streets lined with dignified, historic houses and few people. To the east, I gawked at the variety of shops and restaurants selling goods and food from places I'd never been. In Adams Morgan, they all came together—young, old, poor, rich, local, and from faraway—to gather in restaurants amidst exotic aromas, dance in bars to foreign yet familiar beats, and show off their latest creations in the spaces between buildings.

After hours of riding, I locked the bike to a light pole and descended the stairs into a narrow dark bar called the Asylum. By the time they brought my burger and beer to my booth, I realized I'd picked the right place. Nearly everyone else in there was a bike messenger. As I eavesdropped and watched the messengers come and go, I drifted back twenty years to my days as a San Francisco bike messenger in the 1980s, the heyday of bike messengers before fax machines and emails stripped the industry.

I'd taken the job on a dare. In the fall of 1981, I was walking along Market Street in downtown San Francisco with my friend Sandy, a fellow river guide. She was about my height of five feet six inches, also blond, but short cropped, with a rounder face and freckles. With the river season long over, we were both out of work. I'd just returned from my first trip to Europe "backpacking" and hosteling with a friend I'd worked with at the Fund for Animals. As Sandy and I walked aimlessly along Market Street's wide brick sidewalks gazing up at the tall buildings, I complained that I had to find a job soon, at least to get me through the winter. The Europe trip, though low budget, had drained my meager savings.

While I believed my life was already packed with valuable experience, I knew I lacked anything noteworthy to most employers. I was seventeen years old. I'd received my GED high school diploma the year before. I'd worked as an activist for several environmental and animal welfare organizations including the Fund for Animals, as a kennel worker at the Marin County Humane Society, and as a wildlife rescuer and caregiver at the Marin Wildlife Center. I could also claim to be an expert river guide and hitchhiker. But few employers needed any of that.

"I dare you to do that," Sandy said.

"What?" I had no idea what she had pointed at.

"Wait a minute," she said. "Another will be along soon." She led me to the curb then craned her neck to see over traffic. "There!"

I followed her pointing finger to a speck of a bike and rider rhythmically pedaling our way. He sped by us in a flash of dirty colors, jean vest, chains, and patches, his bike a wreck, dominated by a twisted front basket.

"That!" she said in triumph. "I dare you to become a bike messenger."

Keeping my eyes on the spot where his glints and colors had vanished between stopped cars, I said, "You're on."

The next day I pulled out the San Francisco phonebook and turned to messenger services. I was at my mom's house in Mill Valley, just over the Golden Gate Bridge from the city, where I still stayed when I was in the area. I'd grown up there, if you can call it growing up. My mother had too, because her grandfather had helped to found the town way back when it was only a tent camp next to the lumber mill. I didn't consider it home because my older brother, Steve, still lived at her house, ready to attack me again. I'd learned to escape danger, first from my father, then from my brother. But my mom insisted I stay there, that Steve wouldn't hurt me, even though I knew otherwise.

That morning, my mom was at work as usual and Steve had gone out, so I had the house to myself. I sat cross-legged on my mom's king-sized bed, the autumn sun slanting across her lime-green bed spread, with the thick phonebook opened in front of me, the yellow rotary phone next to it. After calling a handful of messenger companies, I began to wonder if I could fulfill Sandy's dare. Each had mentioned uniforms and filling out forms, resumes and references. Then I called Sparkies Delivery Service.

"Sparkies," a rough, smoker's voice answered.

"You hiring any bike messengers?" I asked.

"Be here at eight tomorrow morning."

"But," I stammered, not ready to commit, "I thought I might come in next week."

"You want the job?"

"Yeah."

"Be here at eight." Click.

Sitting in the Asylum bar in Washington, D.C., I smiled as the various bike messengers filing past brought back my first day at Sparkies twenty years before.

I entered that cave of a garage that opened onto Clementina alley, south of Market, right at eight in the morning having picked the right commuter bus from Mill Valley. To my left, a jumbled bunch of battered bikes lined the wall. To the right, the musty cavern extended back where a few trucks were jacked up for repairs. Right in front of me lay three graffiti-covered picnic tables draped with the seeming relatives of the bike messenger I'd seen a few days before—hair in pink spikes, more patch-covered jean vests, lots of leather and chains. I liked the place immediately. After threading my way past the picnic tables and curious stares, I reached the sliding glass window at the back. A rough face, framed with wild dust-colored curls, smirked back at me from inside the dispatchers' booth, bent nose, his right forearm in a cast. I began filling out the employment form he had silently laid on the shelf for me. He snatched it away before I was finished.

"Pick a bike," he said in the same raspy voice I recognized from the phone. "23 will show you around."

"What?" came an angry shout from the picnic tables. "Mad Dog, you can't stick me with a fucking rookie all day."

"Just the morning, then I'll cut you loose," Mad Dog growled at him. "And be nice."

I definitely ruined 23's morning, hesitating before running red lights, scared to hop off sidewalks, fumbling to park my bike. It wasn't like I was new to bicycling. I'd been riding bikes since I got my first Schwinn on my fifth Christmas—no training wheels, all sparkling purple with white accents and shiny black tires and fenders. I'd snuck it out of the house while the adults were in the kitchen, pointed it down our steep driveway and let it fly, steering it into a bush just before the street. They caught me on my way up the hill to do it again. I was impressed when they showed me it had brakes. That bike became my first means of escape, a contrast from dark to light, from suffocation to freedom. With each year and larger bikes, I rode farther and farther, often with friends, but not depending on them. I'd pedal away any chance I had.

Riding as a bike messenger was not anything like meandering around Mill Valley and Marin, savoring escape. This was pedaling as hard as you could into a cyclone of cars, trucks, buses, anything that could flatten you, and slipping by. At least 23 slipped by. I tended to pedal back hard on the brake just before the collision to watch him disappear in the angry clamor of traffic. When Mad Dog finally gave him the word to let me go, he pedaled hard away from me like I was diseased.

On my own, I started to get the hang of it. Rookies didn't get radios so I had to use the handful of dimes Mad Dog had given me to call in on pay phones, if I didn't manage to beg a phone from a secretary. Mad Dog would give me an address, I'd find an envelope or package there, and I'd take it to where it was addressed. I was getting paid 45 percent of each pickup and delivery I completed—known as one tag. Most were two-dollar tags, so I began to realize why 23 had ridden all out. I wouldn't be making much that day focused on surviving rather than speed. Still, I began to enjoy riding through the city, the canyons of buildings, the hills sloping skyward on one side, quick views of the green-blue bay on the other.

A few hours later, after managing to pick up and deliver several envelopes and packages, I was coasting pretty fast down a hill when the driver of the Toyota pickup in front of me slammed on his brakes and I slammed my basket into the perfect white OYO letters of his tailgate, turning them into a mangled dent. Mad Dog called me in after I'd exchanged the company info with the driver and found a phone. He allowed me the slightest sideways smile the next morning when I strolled into the garage right at eight. I never pointed my front wheel at the back of a car again, always the slot between cars to be ready to lean and slip by if they slammed on their brakes. That week I learned how to ride without wasting energy braking, to slip by and flow through the snarl just as 23 had.

Over the ensuing weeks as I kept showing up ready to ride at eight o'clock, the other messengers made room for me at the picnic tables and held out their palms as we flew past each other in the streets—high-speed high-fives. Each had their own distinct howl so I always knew who was nearby even if buildings were between us. I came up with my own—starting like a high-pitched coyote and ending with a chattering ay-kay-kay-kay.

We sliced through that city, disgusted with the moronic drivers and sloths that dripped off the sidewalks into our paths. We were a menace and proud of it, and because we were feared, we feared no one, saw no one, just ebbs and flows of moving objects to cut through.

Nob Hill is the highest, steepest hill in downtown, five sheer blocks broken only by the short ledges of cross streets. A delivery to the top meant a challenge to ride as far up California Street as I could, trying to break my last record before checking over my shoulder for the next cable car to grab onto for a tug up the final blocks. My first few descents of California from the top of Nob cooked my coaster brake hub until I noticed the lights turned green in sequence. After a few rough trials I learned to perch at the brink of the hill until the second light turned green, then pedal hard and tuck into the plummet turning myself and bike into an unstoppable projectile. If my timing was off, the wall of pedestrians at the next cross street wouldn't have opened yet. I'd yell, "No brakes!" and miraculously a gap would appear.

I developed a last-ditch maneuver for times when the pedestrian wall didn't open, but fortunately never needed it on a descent of Nob Hill. Pedaling all out mid-block I'd watch the next light, anticipating the red. I never stopped for reds, just leaned to the right to weave through the cross traffic—parallel, never perpendicular. But before I could do that lean, I had to make it through the pedestrians closing in from each side. The first time a gap closed on me I instinctively rolled to my left laying my bike down, sparks flying from my pedal as my tires nudged the scattering shoes. I polished that move as a reliable backup.

Those few city dwellers who dared to defy us became our playthings. We'd chase down bus drivers who cut us off to grab the back cables that held their electrical arms to the wires over the street. A hard yank and pull and the bus would drift to a stop and we'd pedal past, taunting.

Taxi drivers were our other archenemies, always good for an amusing clash. One made the mistake of tapping me with his fender then gunning it, thinking he could get away. I raced after him slipping one red to catch him stopped at the next. I coasted up to his passenger side, opened the front door wide, then the back, then coasted over to his side and opened that back door, all the while cursing him through the openings. The light turned green and he couldn't move, couldn't even get out to close his doors because he'd land right in my spitting face. Traffic honked and edged around his doors. Spectators on each corner clapped and whistled. I let the light turn red before pedaling away, watching over my shoulder as he meekly got out and closed the doors.

If we couldn't find easy fun amongst the crowds, we'd turn on each other, the best prank hiding another messenger's bike before they returned from a delivery. Bursting out of a building, ready to jump on my bike, I'd gape at the vacant space where I had parked. My messenger buds got me good several times. It always took me a moment, then I'd start checking around corners or behind dumpsters to find it in easy range. The longest search finally ended when I looked up and found my bike in a tree.

One day a guy, looking like any other businessman or "suit" as we referred to them, gave me hope that maybe some of these sloths had a spark of life just like us. I had brushed his arm as I hopped a curb onto a sidewalk downtown. The brush was so light I figured he hadn't even noticed. So I put all my focus into pulling off another move I'd been working on—approaching the door of a building with a perfectly smooth wall on the right side of it, I'd check just enough of my speed then ease my handlebar into the wall until it barely touched. As it slid along the wall, I'd lift my right leg over the seat, step off, and run alongside my bike. If I'd set it up well, the bike would stop just before the entry and I'd cut in front to lunge through the door.

That day, I had it all lined up perfectly. This was going to be one of my best yet. But as I lifted my leg, swaying there in that precarious ballerina position, that crafty suit swept up and kicked the bike right out from under me. I crumbled into a heap tangled in my bike, my pedal gouging my back as I looked up in wonder at his amused face. Then I burst out laughing.

"Good one," I said when I finally caught my breath. "You got me."

But my laughter wiped his amusement into a scowl and he marched away.

I got hooked on the job, riding ten hours a day and only going back to my mom's house to sleep. Eventually they bumped me up to 50 percent commission for riding fast. Over seven winters I refined my skills, rarely touching the brake, to become one of Sparkies' fastest—Cream Cheese (dubbed by Pig), number 31—until a Cadillac blew out my knee and ended my career. Workman's compensation insurance paved the way for me to start my bike shop in Prescott, Arizona, where I'd gone to college and found many friends. I opened the doors in the fall of 1991, as close to being a suit as I'd ever been.

That evening, a decade later in Washington, D.C., Karen and I finally had a chance to meet at her one-room, one-bedroom, street-level apartment. With cold beer bottles in hand—me sitting at the small table at the window enjoying the pedestrians sidling by a few feet away as Karen fussed with her rotund cat Minnie—we filled each other in on our lives and how we'd come to be in D.C. She was from upstate New York and had come there to work on environmental policy. When I told her I'd found the Asylum, she swore I must have a bike messenger radar because that was their main hangout, one of her favorite bars for meeting her bike messenger friends. She didn't mind that I'd named her bike Fifi to capture her French elegance.

Over the next three days, I rode Fifi around that stunning city—from close neighborhoods to towering monuments—attending bike advocacy strategy meetings and lobbying Congress with other bike advocates from around the country. Some I recognized from Philadelphia, though I was just as likely to spark a conversation with others. The chill from Thunderhead leaders remained, but I didn't let it sour my trip. I was sorry to park Fifi in Karen's basement on the morning I left, even with a strange certainty that I'd be back to ride her again.

Back in Prescott, I returned to pushing our local bike projects. Prescott Alternative Transportation (PAT) was only four years old, but already we'd accomplished impressive wins for bicycling and walking—a new greenway trail along our downtown creeks was under construction, bike lanes had been striped, and the city's first bike plan had been approved.

These wins for my town had intensified my devotion to bicycle advocacy as the new paths and lanes buzzed to life with pedalers—each bike a car left at home or never bought, a kid moving by their own power. Each rider breathing in and engaging with our community, which can't be done from inside a car.

I'd ended up in Prescott, Arizona nearly twenty years before when my battered Toyota Corona broke down in the spring of 1982 on a cross country journey with my friend Sue from Boston. She had told me over the phone that she'd never seen the Pacific Ocean, so I took a break from my job as a bike messenger to drive across, pick her up, and deliver her to the ocean I knew so well. I was eighteen then with several long hitchhiking trips already under my belt. So a spur-of-the moment drive across the country was nothing.

After the car broke down, Sue and I met a guy who let us sleep on the floor of his trailer for a whole week as we waited for the part. He showed us around Prescott, including the progressive little university called Prescott College. As a proud high school dropout, I'd missed much of the basics and this was becoming frustrating especially in Europe trying to hold conversations with other teenagers who knew far more about the world.

High school had proven to be a farce by my freshman year when I found Western Civilization for the third time on my schedule since I'd first taken it in eighth grade. When I complained, the administrator told me they were doing me a favor because I could reuse the maps and papers I had done for the two previous courses. After that, I spent my days in Sacramento lobbying with the Fund for Animals or at the humane society or wildlife center caring for animals. I even joined a marsh preservation effort fighting a development in the marsh across from the high school. During investigative trips wading through the salty mud and pickleweed I fantasized that I was an escaped prisoner toying with my would-be captors inside the yellowed towers across the road. Those captors soon assigned me to a program for likely drop-outs. And then I obliged.

By the time the car part arrived in Prescott, this high-desert town of forty thousand had won my heart with its perfect mix of diehard westerners and hippie artists set at nearly six thousand feet and surrounded on three sides by the mountains of central Arizona. I started at Prescott College in January 1983, a semester each year, connecting with many dear friends, students and teachers. I even married one. Jim Knaup and I always seemed to be the last two hanging around the keg at college parties, so I suppose it was inevitable. He's also hard to miss with his bushy beard, infectious beer-belly laughs, and talent for pranks.

Later I attended Yavapai College, Prescott's community college, and Old Dominion University's extension there, for history, languages, social studies, welding, and civil engineering. Most profound for my bicycle advocacy efforts, I learned that engineers love to solve problems. You simply need to give them the right problem to solve—not how to move more cars faster, but how to create streets where bicyclists and pedestrians are prioritized. They eat it up.

Even as I honed my skills at the local level, I craved more. More impact. More reach from the national level. To be part of the action that touched every community, every street. A dangerous craving like love or addiction.

My next opportunity came in July 2001, the annual gathering of the Thunderhead Alliance, this time in the eastern Cascade Mountains. This would also be my third attempt at a Bike Hunt. While Fifi had been a triumph in her own way, I was determined to return to the concept I'd started in Philadelphia—hunt down that kind person who could help me find an affordable used bike.

I'd flown into Wenatchee, Washington on the earliest plane I could catch out of Seattle after traveling from Prescott that day. I didn't need to be at the mountain resort until that evening. Even though there was no rush, I didn't want to miss any of the sessions that would include the latest methods of improving communities with bicycle provisions. The resort was about an hour's bus ride away with regular bus service, so I figured I had about four hours to find a bike. No problem. At that point I hadn't learned the important Bike Hunt rule that the hunt always takes all the time you have.

Wenatchee is a long, narrow city of about thirty thousand, squeezed between the Columbia River on the east and the foothills of the Cascade Mountains on the west. The airport sits at the southern tip. So, being a diligent bike hunter, I got off at the first stop of the airport shuttle bus to explore every potential. Suffice it to say I saw that *whole* city, tip to tip. I went into every pawn shop, every thrift store, every shop that sold anything with wheels, and hunted down all three bike shops. Wenatchee, it appeared, didn't have one used bike for sale.

By the time I had trudged the length of the city and was approaching the final bike shop at the very north end, it was a dead heat as to which would give out first, my legs or the time I had left. My backpack felt like a building as I willed each foot forward. Three hours and nothing. On top of that, this last bike shop wasn't even a bike shop, but some sort of sports and fitness center. As if they'd have a cheap used bike amongst all their weight lifting equipment.

The exterior dampened my hope all the more—flat stucco beige walls with a bright red plastic sign, the building stuck like chewed gum in the middle of a sea of asphalt. My decision that day to enter that unlikely place followed the Bike Hunt rule I'd discovered in D.C. of never limiting yourself to places where you think you'll find your bike.

Leaning on the counter, exhausted, hardly caring why they'd chosen to hang treadmills from the soaring ceiling, I didn't notice the slender, styled redhead at first. She had moved to the counter from nowhere. It wasn't until she asked about her bike that I woke up. Bike. That's what I'm looking for. Still too exhausted to speak, I chose instead to listen. The chipper young man got her information and brought out her bike. As they discussed her repair bill, I took my chance and broke in.

"Hey, so I'm looking for a used bike." This was about the three-thousandth time that day I'd said this. But this time I wasn't going to let go. One of these two had to help me.

Maybe my desperation came through in my voice as I explained my predicament because the lady declared she could help. Her daughter had left her old bike behind when she'd left for college. She'd love to sell it to me. Reenergized by hope, I climbed into her pickup truck for the ride into the foothills where she lived.

Fighting my inner struggle between always being polite in someone else's home and my near panic about the time, I fidgeted in her garage as she told me the story of the bike, how her daughter had tired of it and left it there. It was fine, nothing special—a girl's-frame fifteen-speed mountain bike, well cared for, bright purple, everything there and well tuned. Finally she accepted my money. I threw on my pack, grabbed the grips, and took the pedals. As I shot out of the garage, she shouted to turn left at such and such street. I yelled my thanks, waving back as best I could as I pedaled into the downhill pull of gravity.

I made it to the bus stop in minutes, covering the same distance that had taken me hours to walk. As I caught my breath and waited for the bus driver to open the doors, I dubbed my new ride the Purple Flash.

I sat at the front of the bus gazing out through the windshield and Purple Flash's handlebar where she perched in the bus's bike rack. We traversed a lush valley above the banks of a shimmering river. I got off at the village noted in the travel instructions and pedaled Purple Flash over a wooden bridge that crossed the river, stopping for a few minutes to pretend I was scouting a run through the whitewater. In such a setting—the river, the sheer, snow-striped mountains, the pine trees—I was sure to experience a special weekend.

I rode into the resort with its glamorous, mountain-themed buildings dotted around the forest and found the first session finishing in a cabin near the entry. I joined the group as they filed toward the main lodge for drinks and banter before dinner, catching up, glad to be there. Over the next few days, though, the sessions lacked inspiration. I met familiar faces, but my hope for new friendships faded into stiff discussions, the board chair always watching. Fortunately, Karen was there and we managed to find fun in every activity. Then came the crowning end to the trip—my first bike giveaway.

At that point in my development of the Bike Hunt, I hadn't even considered the giveaway. I was still acting on my primal need for a bike when attending bike meetings, to have a bike, not just talk about them. Even that early seed of the Bike Hunt had begun to replace the connection to people that I had already missed in the bicycle movement. I had experienced something similar lobbying for the Fund for Animals. If I hadn't returned each weekend to my shifts at the Marin Humane Society and Marin Wildlife Center, if I hadn't listened to my internal need to hold, comfort, and attend to suffering animals, my passion would have died along with my ability to lobby. From the start, the Bike Hunt had kept my passion kindled even as my delusion with national bicycle advocacy unraveled. But hunting for a bike was only part of it. In fact, the hunt wasn't whole until I discovered the giveaway.

It was the afternoon before I had to leave the mountain village above Wenatchee, Washington. Our group of bike advocates had dwindled to about a dozen who had lingered for an extra few days after the retreat ended. We had just returned from a bike ride to a deep, blue swimming hole surrounded by craggy mountain peaks. We were lounging behind the bed and breakfast where we were staying, on the back steps, in chairs, and in the grass, Purple Flash sitting pretty right in the middle of the lawn. I dared one of the advocates to try popping a wheelie with her (I'd never ridden a better wheelie bike). He took me up on it and pedaled her across the vast sloping lawn that wove between leafy trees down to the rippling, boulder-strewn river. I was sitting on the back porch steps near the owner of the bed and breakfast. She had come out to enjoy the fading orange of the sunset with us.

As I watched Purple Flash in action, the ball finally dropped. What was I going to do with her when I left the next morning? I can't claim a spark of genius or even inspiration. It was more like a sorry process of elimination as I considered the remoteness of the location and glanced around at the visiting faces. Finally my troubled gaze fell on our hostess. She was middle-aged, slightly overweight, but with a strong ruggedness that fit the setting. Bingo. I asked her if she wanted Purple Flash.

Her forceful guffaw was followed by a rapid list of reasons why she could never accept the bike, all delivered as the two of us watched Purple Flash dance and slide around the lawn. She hadn't ridden a bike in thirty years. Her husband was ill, so he wouldn't be able to join her on rides. She knew a few women in town who rode, but she could never keep up with them. There were too many gears on the bike, which she could never figure out. Her last bike had had pedal brakes, so she was sure to crash if she tried to use those handlebar brakes. Despite her barrage of objections, I knew I'd found a home for Purple Flash.

I got up and called the guy over. He gladly dismounted when I explained what I was up to. She stood, still offering excuses, but softer and slower as I pushed the handlebar to her. I knew she had to touch it if this was going to work. As soon as her hand rested on the handlebar grip her excuses turned to inquiries.

"How would I shift gears if I took this bike?"

I moved the bike so she could see the gears and showed her how the shifter on the right moved the rear derailleur to change the gears. As I moved the shifter, I explained that those five gears were the ones that made smaller adjustments in speed. The shifter on the left moved the front derailleur through the front three gears, and all she had to do with that was choose the best for the overall terrain. It was already in the middle gear, so I told her she wouldn't even have to touch it until she was comfortable shifting the right one.

"What about the brakes? I've heard horror stories about people crashing with these brakes."

Here was my opportunity to seal the deal. I explained that she'd need to stand over the bike as if ready to ride in order for me to show her properly. When she did, I had her practice squeezing the right lever first because that lever worked the rear brake. As long as the rear brake was engaged before the front brake, she wouldn't have to worry about crashing because of the brakes.

That was all she needed. Without warning she set her foot on the pedal, jumped onto the seat, and pedaled out from under me. I ran to catch up, but lost sight of her around the building until I rounded the corner. There she was, sailing like the breeze around the expansive circular driveway before disappearing behind the landscaped island in the middle. After long, anxious seconds, she reappeared, banked easily around and headed toward me with the slightest sway as if she were dancing. I thought she would stop, so I was ready to congratulate her and continue the lesson, but she whisked right by me like I wasn't even there, her sways turning to wide swoops that took up the width of the driveway. As she disappeared behind the landscaped island again, I heard a strange sound flowing back from the surrounding pine trees—she was singing!

2
I'm In

The frigid pre-dawn air smacked me as I stepped through the sliding glass hotel entry rolling Rebel at my side. Had I not had this urgent errand, I would have turned right around and headed back to my cozy room to wait out the hour before the airport shuttle would arrive. One hour to scan the unfamiliar streets of downtown Denver for the proper recipient of Rebel—a worn, but sturdy mountain bike I'd bought at a pawn shop two days before. October 2001, an early winter. This was the wrap up of my fourth Bike Hunt, my first deliberate giveaway. Pony, in Philadelphia, had inspired the hunt. Fifi, in D.C., had broadened my expectations. And Purple Flash, in Wenatchee, had sweetened it all with her giveaway. I had to get this one right.

I'd been riding Rebel to the various meetings scheduled around a transportation summit for western officials and advocates. He was a good bike, brakes a bit sketchy, but he rolled smooth, shifted well, and actually came to a stop if I squeezed both levers hard. His blue paint was scratched through in many spots though I could see he was once a looker. The pawn shop owner had lent me the few tools I needed to tighten his hubs, adjust his stem, and rethread the left pedal that had nearly fallen off. I named him Rebel because he had obviously faced great odds, but he had a certain vigor to him as soon as I pedaled off, as if he'd hated being cooped up in that pawn shop.

I donned my helmet (a bad habit I had back then) and started pedaling, fighting the urge to pedal fast against the cold. Granules of snow pelted my face and sugarcoated the few people out, walking fast, pre-rush hour. Even though this was my first deliberate Bike Hunt giveaway, I knew Rebel's new owner could be anyone I passed. I needed to take it slow, study each face, find the one with a bit of sadness, something missing in their life.

I turned onto the 16th Street Mall where I'd seen homeless people the night before laying out their blankets in doorways. The 16th Street Mall was formerly a traffic-filled city street, but it no longer admitted cars, only pedestrians, cyclists, and a free tram that moseyed down the center. This allowed me to zig and zag from doorway to doorway across the street and back. But I kept striking out. All I could see were mounds of blankets, cardboard, and newspaper with a bit of sugarcoating for effect. Come to think of it, if I'd slept in a doorway the night before, I sure as heck wouldn't be throwing back my blankets anytime soon either, at least not until the sun was well up. And I wasn't about to go up and nudge any of the mounds. Picture that: Nudge, "Hiya, do you want a bicycle?" Let's just say that wasn't an option.

I checked my watch—only half an hour before I had to be back at the hotel in time to grab my things and bolt to the shuttle. The farther I went, the longer it would take to walk back. I was nearing the end of the pedestrian mall area with only the endless expanse of the unfamiliar city stretching beyond. I shook off the thought of failure.

Only three doorways with mounds remained before I'd have to venture out into the untamed streets. As my heart sank with the prospect of traveling too far to walk back in time for my shuttle, I glanced to my right down a side street at an eerie scene. In the beam of a streetlamp, a billow of ghostly steam whirled up against the descending snow. At first, all I saw was the steam, then a dark shape and then all seven of them, palms pushing down as they rocked back and forth.

Standing on my pedals, squeezing hard on the brake levers, I nearly fell over as Rebel eased to a stop. It took all my will not to ride full speed right at them and tell them how excited I was to find them. I carefully eased my leg over the seat, composed myself, and walked as nonchalantly as I could toward the group. They were about half a block away, time enough for me to practice my line, and then I realized I had a big problem—what if they all wanted Rebel? I stopped. No, it was my last chance. Time was evaporating with each hesitation.

With careful steps forward I studied the group. They were Native American, likely a family, four generations. There was a boy, maybe four or five, too small for Rebel. There was an old woman, grey streaks in her long black hair held back with a turquoise-inlaid clasp, and an old man with a black cowboy hat and deep grooves in his face. They wouldn't want him, would they? A middle-aged man draped with a colorful blanket hardly looked up, unlikely to get involved. That left the three who looked to be in their teens and twenties, one girl, the others guys. Still a problem. I kept moving, much less excited than a few minutes before. I decided to let it play out and follow my instincts, bail if I needed to.

I walked right toward them along the sidewalk, carefully watching each face through the dancing billows of steam, especially the three. The old man stepped back, shielding the old woman. The kid squeezed between their legs. The three stood their ground. I kept walking. About ten feet from them I stopped.

"Hi," I said, and that's all.

I waited. But I didn't have to wait long. One of the young men—maybe seventeen, Broncos team jacket, shoulder-length black hair, inquisitive expression—stepped forward.

"Hi," he said. "How's it going?"

Problem solved. He would get Rebel. I delivered my story directly to him, not the others. I explained that I'd bought the bike to ride during a conference, but I needed to find him a home before I left that morning. He listened carefully with his eyes on Rebel.

"How much you want for it?"

"Nothing, except your promise to take good care of him. I named him Rebel." I wasn't sure if I should have said this, but when he looked up at me and smiled, I was glad I had.

"I'll take good care of him, I promise," he said as he reached out to touch the handlebar grip. I let go, so he had to grab it before the bike fell.

"He's all yours."

He swung his new bike to his side, then crouched down to look at the wheels and gears.

"How many gears?"

"Eighteen. The brakes are a bit worn, but if you use both at the same time it's no problem. He rides real smooth."

With that he stood and turned to the group, showing them his new ride. Though his back was to me, his elation was reflected in their faces. Then I remembered the lock, a new detail I'd added for this Bike Hunt. I'd brought an inexpensive coil lock to give away with the bike so the recipient wouldn't have to worry about it getting stolen. The lock was dangling from the back of the seat, the key still in my pocket. I fished for it and brought it out.

"I almost forgot, you'll need the key to the lock."

He turned around, looked down at my outstretched hand and back up into my face as if I'd offered him *another* million dollars. He took the key, speechless.

That was it. Success. I was about to turn to leave when the old man, hidden behind the steam, abruptly spoke.

"Wait," he said as he stepped through the group to face me, his hand strangely patting his hat. The young man with Rebel was still smiling so I knew this wasn't a threat. "Can you give my grandson a hat too?"

It took me a minute to figure out what he was saying. A helmet, he wanted me to give his grandson a helmet.

"No," I said, now also patting my helmeted head. "I only have this one. I'm sorry."

"That's okay," he said and paused to admire the bike with his grandson. "Thanks for the bike. He needs it. He's looking for a job this week and this will help him. We need the money as you can see." Then he slipped back behind the steam.

I wished the young man good luck on his job hunt and in reply he held out his right fist. I'd never seen this before, but instinctively I made a fist and touched it to his before turning and

I'm In | 35

walking away.

A few weeks after Rebel's mystical giveaway in Denver, I was riding Fifi through Washington, D.C. It was early November 2001 and I was just sinking into the seductive spell of D.C. politics.

I'd been invited to join the founding board of a new coalition of national bicycle advocacy organizations called America Bikes, so I'd made the trip to D.C. for our first board meeting. Even as I'd focused my work on the bike shop and bike advocacy in Prescott, I'd been doing my best to participate in national activities, mostly through remote committee work, and it seemed to have paid off with this invitation.

I had found a bike advocate in Arlington, Virginia, just across the Potomac River, who would let me stay at her place since Karen had another guest staying with her. Karen and I had connected at her apartment for beers and stories that afternoon when I picked up Fifi. At that point I hadn't fully separated the astonishing beauty of the city from the snarled politics I was delving into. Both were still new and exciting. Thanks to Karen and Fifi, I learned that Washington is a city apart from petty politics.

Even knowing this, I was drawn to the intoxication of latent power. That night I left Union Station and let Fifi fly down Capitol Hill, slicing through the slots between backed-up cars before banking left onto the National Mall where the delirium of the place pulled me to a stop. The full moon spotlit the Capitol building behind me and the Washington Monument in front. They glowed a purpley white, each tugging at me, holding me in place as I absorbed the sight of one, then the other and back.

I had just had dinner at Union Station with a small group of national bicycle advocates, some of my fellow founders of America Bikes, the conversation a giddy seriousness about what we would make Congress do for bikes. I believed it. And I believed I would play a major role in the fable we scribbled that night. I had no reason for doubt since I'd sat through many similar meetings in Sacramento as we had planned our lobbying strategies for animal rights.

Our table was near the center of the spacious barrel-vaulted area of the station only separated from the crowds by a low fence. As we were choosing our seats, I had approached one of the advocates who was from Colorado to tell her about Rebel and my successful Bike Hunt only a few weeks prior in her home state. Before I got past my discovery of Rebel at the pawn shop she stopped me. There was no time for such silly stories amidst national bicycle politics. I let it pass and relished the dinner and political discussions that charged my ride down Capitol Hill and onto the moonlit National Mall.

"I'm here!" I said out loud to the Capitol. "I'm in!" I told the Washington Monument and set out toward it. I had found a route on my map that snaked through the monuments then across a bridge over the Potomac to the place I was staying in Arlington. I stopped to look directly up from the base of the Washington Monument then pedaled down its grassy mound, across 17th Street and onto the straight path that leads to the Lincoln Memorial. I glimpsed Lincoln through the tree branches then slowed to meander through the sharp patterns their shadows cut across the path, the Reflecting Pool shimmering in the moonlight to my left, the dark of the wooded park nudging my right.

I locked Fifi at the bottom of the mountainous stairway before making the climb. It was nearly midnight, so I was the only flesh and blood person around. At the threshold of the monument I stopped as if asking President Lincoln for permission to enter and was struck by the gentle greeting in his face. Sidling over to the ceiling-to-floor words chiseled into the lofty inside walls of the monument, I did my best to absorb what he must have meant, but soon moved back to face him where I found far more meaning in his expression. This great man and I were born on the same day—February 12th—a point of pride since my earliest days as an activist.

With only three months until I hit thirty-eight, I thought I had found my best opportunity for contributing yet—the bicycle movement. The animal rights movement had been too driven by revenge. I grew tired of explaining why hurting those who hurt animals was wrong. The environmental movement was too detached from people and communities.

The bicycle advocacy movement seemed just right with its focus on remolding communities for everyone and everything that lived there. We'd bring freedom of movement to people of all incomes, ages, and abilities. Streets would be reshaped into public spaces so forgiving that any skittish dog would survive a reckless leap into traffic. Trees and plants would be planted where asphalt had once stifled the soil. And streams would be released from pipes and concrete channels to become the focal points of linear parks and urban trail systems. The bicycle movement seemed to reach every cause via a simple, unthreatening machine. That night, facing Lincoln as his peer, I believed I had found my way to change the world.

Back on Fifi, I pedaled around the side of his memorial and across the bridge over the Potomac. Under the shadow of trees on the other side, I caught a glimpse of a bike path sign and an arrow to the left, placed exactly at the turn for the path, no warning. Speed unchecked, I made my decision and leaned hard into the dark, feeling only with the tires. Fifi and I rose up an invisible embankment as I leaned harder, fighting against soft ground that grabbed at the tires. Then I felt the firm grip of the path, leaned back into a straight up position, and stood on my pedals howling as I used to as a bike messenger when I'd barely escaped a bloody death in traffic.

I released the adrenaline through my pedal strokes, still standing on the pedals and whisking the bike under me with each stroke. Over a rise I was still riding the evening's exhilaration when the sight of the Pentagon plowed into me. Enormous floodlights turned the scene into a miniature daytime adding to my brain's scrambled interpretation. This was a toy Pentagon slashed by an imaginary monster. As I coasted closer, reality sunk in. The five-sided building loomed above the trees and covered an area as large as a city neighborhood. The gash in its side was the size of a city block, the black char spreading far beyond the gash to scar that entire side of the gargantuan building.

I let Fifi glide forward, now along a sidewalk that hugged the road in front of the Pentagon, my eyes fixed on the destruction. I had to glance ahead now and then to stay on the narrow ledge of concrete. That's how I discovered the impromptu memorial. At first it looked like a pile of litter, but as I approached I realized it was a scattered collection of cards and flowers stuck into the ground on a gentle slope of grass next to the sidewalk. I stood reading those cards, my back to the Pentagon, trying to understand the loss that newscasts could never capture.

Gracie, you'll always be with me. Your loving husband.

We'll never forget you, Tom! Marge, Sam, Alice, and the dogs.

Maxine, our world is less without you. (Just hearts and kisses for a signature.)

The simple cards pulled me back to a world where kindness and love tried to deflect monsters. Standing there with those cards, glancing back at the gash in the Pentagon, I saw my father punch my mother's face. Her tall, delicate form fell against the window seat and he pushed her down punching again and again, her mahogany hair splayed out, framing her terrified, reddened face. I saw me and my brother Steve shouting from the upstairs balcony for her to swing back, for her to win the fight, though we knew it was hopeless. I saw our family albums held in my mom's lap as she told me about the trips they'd enjoyed together before my brother and I were born. I heard the love in her voice even as she screamed for him to stop punching.

I saw my father storm through our backdoor into the kitchen and head straight to the martini shaker. Those were the few minutes in a day I saw my father sober. He had his own, failing law practice, but wanted to be a writer. That rattle of ice taught me to run to my room because if I watched too long, I'd see the warping. I think that's why I related to the Incredible Hulk cartoon. I could see it happen to my father any evening.

I stood with my brother Steve swapping dreams. He'd told me that most nights he dreamed of jumping to his death, though he always woke too soon. I tended to fly in my dreams, sweeping through forests and out across mountains, careening through cities, and buzzing friends. I promised that that night I'd try jumping instead of flying if he'd try flying. We shook on it. In my dream, I was entertaining a bunch of my friends from school. We were in my upstairs bedroom playing with my toys. Then I remembered my promise and told everyone I had to leave, went to the window and jumped. I woke before hitting, just as Steve had promised I would. Steve forgot to fly.

I felt the cowering, my knees to my chest, the hard floor and the cold porcelain of the toilet the night the three of us ran from my father, upstairs, not out. We chose the upstairs bathroom, my mother locking the door with shaking hands as my father pounded, pounded, pounded that he would kill us all. Steve found the corner behind the toilet. I took the other side, right below the window glancing up, wondering how much it would hurt if I jumped. We huddled there for hours after the silence, my mother sitting on the lid trying to sooth us by stroking our hair.

I saw that morning of my eighth birthday, greeted with birthday wishes by my mother as I came out of my bedroom.

"Where's Daddy?" I asked, as I always did in order to get a bead on where the danger lurked.

"He's gone to England," she said, as if it was down the block.

"When is he coming back?" I asked, still on alert.

"Probably never."

"Good," I said. "What's for breakfast?" I still remember saying that, cool as a cucumber. Good. What's for breakfast? I'm proud of saying that because it eased my mother's strain into a grin. She didn't have to sleep with a knife under her pillow anymore.

My relief didn't last long. Something changed in my brother after Dad left. I noticed it the morning my mom went to her new job, her first job since before they'd married. We lived in an immense four-bedroom house on a sycamore-lined, narrow street in Mill Valley, proof of my father's delusion of wealth. When he left, my mom opened the threatening letters addressed to him. Bankruptcy was imminent, the house soon to be the bank's. She took the secretary job at a real estate firm on the edge of town hoping to fend them off. She invited strangers into our house to insult our stuff before handing her some money and leaving with their chosen books or antiques.

That morning she left for her new job, Steve and I ran to the side windows to watch her back our brown station wagon out of the garage and drive away down our long driveway.

He turned and attacked me.

Every weekday after that, I hid from him, but he'd usually find me. Older than me by a year and a half and a hand taller, also blond, he made a menacing foe, even though we were both kids—eight and not yet ten. I'd run through the immense house with him close behind wielding the fireplace poker. Finally one day I ran outside. I pulled my purple girl-sized Schwinn out of the garage and rode down our driveway onto the narrow street and away. Sometimes I'd go to my friend Greg's house and we'd find something fun to do, usually riding bikes or walking the creeks that threaded behind the buildings of our town. When school was in session, I tried not to go back to the house until well after dark when I was sure my mom would be there to protect me. These bike and creek adventures soon became my choice for weekends too.

Sometimes I'd bring my tennis racket and ride to the Mill Valley Tennis Club where my mom had taught me to play not long after I'd learned how to walk. She'd spent much of her youth there too, not as an escape, but for pure tennis passion. Her parents, my grandparents, Helen and Stewart Bostwick, had founded the club back in the 1920s on a triangular wedge of land between steep, wooded hills. After raising funds from about fifty founding members and securing a loan, they built a small swimming pool at the point, then the five courts in the widest part. The slender brown-shingled clubhouse fit tight between the courts and access road, its court side all windows, seating, and perches, designed for fans of the game. Sometimes, if I could arrange a game, we'd play through dusk until the ball would disappear between our rackets. If I couldn't get a game, I'd sit on the wide wooden bench that ran the length of the courts and watch the action.

After holding the bank back for about a year, my mom called

my father's brother, our Uncle Den. Maybe she figured that Den would feel some responsibility for the mess his brother had left behind. More likely, my mom knew Den's caring nature and that at least he could offer ideas. I remember Den's visit as a relieving break, which allowed me to stay at the house as he and my mom talked, Den's warm eyes concerned. He was as tall as my father, but with a narrower, fitter build, his wavy brown hair accentuating the kind lines of his face. My mom brightened up too, cooking fancy meals she couldn't afford.

After Den left, we had to leave too. He managed to prevent bankruptcy, but the bank got the house. We moved in with my grandmother, who lived alone in a quaint little house about three short blocks away on Walnut Avenue. Though her real name was Helen, we called her Mimi. She was stout by then since she could no longer play tennis, and wore her long grey-blond hair in a bun. Steve and I shared one of the two rooms in the attic. My mom had the other. During those long months living as a guest, Steve behaved himself. It helped that Mimi was home most of the time. She had a whimsical way about her, always looking for unusual activities for us. She showed us how to make mud pies with her bread pans in the creek behind her house, then build things with them when they dried. Some mornings she'd present a letter to us, written during the night by Mr. Rat who lived in the attic with us. Before going to bed, she'd place a blank piece of paper in her old black typewriter that had long keys like fingers. If this mysterious creature had been touched by his muse, she'd have a letter to share with us, usually about his escapades, but if we'd behaved badly, Mr. Rat included words of wisdom for improvement. Even though I adored Mimi and her entertainments, by then I had chosen my freedom to roam and continued my daily adventures, which gave me real stories to share with her.

Not long after we moved in with her, Mimi started looking for other ways I could spend my energy. She signed me up as a volunteer for a group that was responsible for the health of Mill Valley's street trees. In the main part of town that sits in the valley, every street has a tree name and the trees that line them match their street name. I was assigned Elm, Catalpa, and Locust, and walked them with my clipboard once a week looking for disease and injury.

Later, Mimi signed me up as a volunteer at the Marin County Humane Society (she was one of its founders), which became a paid job and led to my other roles in the animal rights movement.

Uncle Den's solution for our homelessness was to buy a small house one block away from Mimi's, also on Walnut. My mother was clearly embarrassed by this charity. On his next visit to complete the sale, he assured her over and over that he was pleased to make the investment with his children, my cousins, in mind even as he promised she could live in the house as long as she needed to. She insisted on paying rent. This troubled him, but they finally agreed that she'd pay two hundred dollars a month, which he never changed up to his death more than twenty years later. Two hundred dollars a month for a two-story, three-bedroom house in what has become one of the highest-priced places to live in the country.

We moved in on April 10, 1974. I remember that date because I wrote it in pen inside a petal of the flowered wallpaper that covered the tiny kitchen. Mom yelled at me from the sink about five feet across from me as I sat at the table-for-two wedged against the wall inscribing the year. Too late. That made me ten and two months old.

Once we settled in, Steve settled back into violence. My room was to the left at the top of the stairs, his was down the hall to the right, beyond Mom's room. To get into my room, you took a step down and opened the door at your left again, the room extending back the way you'd come up the stairs. This complex entry was part of why I chose that room. It felt more protected. I covered the walls and ceiling with pictures of animals, boats, and faraway places. On the ceiling above my bed, I stapled a map of the world so I could trace trips with my finger.

On non-school days and after I dropped out, when I didn't manage to escape in time, I'd listen for his hard step down, his reaching for my door knob that had no lock. I'd bought a cheap

Pakistani sword at a swap meet and hung it by its red velvet sheath from the ceiling above my bed. When I heard his angry step accompanied by threats of pounding me, I'd reach for the sword and sit on the edge of my bed at the far end of my room with the sword unsheathed in my lap. I learned that the sight of the sword kept him on the door side of the room. These were the times I heard his side of the story.

He'd gaze at the sword, deciding what to do, then slump down to the floor cross-legged, his head in his hands, blond hair spilling between his long fingers. He'd come to hurt me, but switched to needing me. Through blubbering sobs, he would explain why it was time for him to kill himself. I'd sit in silence until he looked up, seeking something from me. I'd explain that Dad had left all of us, not just him, that he had nice friends at school who liked him, that he'd find something interesting to do with his life, that he was smart and could offer his talents in many roles. Finally I'd set down my sword, offer him my hand, and coax him outside to look at the sky and the trees. There was an enormous redwood tree in our backyard and sometimes I'd talk him into climbing it with me to get a better view of life and the world. We could see most of the town from its tip—Mount Tamalpais cradling the picturesque downtown on one end, the wooded ridges that formed the valley extending to the bay, and a peek at the tip of San Francisco's buildings. It would have been a nice place to grow up.

After I got my driver's license and bought a beat-up, dull green Toyota Corona for two hundred dollars, I'd coax him to take a drive with me. We'd go to the beach at Fort Cronkite to walk along the rolling water's edge in the fog and grey, then climb up above the steep rocky cliffs. I'd continue my sales pitch for life as he'd peer over the cliffs seeming to admire their finality.

The day after a climb of the redwood or a drive to the beach, if I hadn't escaped in time, he'd ambush me again, often leaving welts on my arms or legs with whatever implement he'd chosen.

Fortunately, he kept his attacks on my mother to psychological torture like barrages of threats and locking her out of the house to scream curses at her from his bedroom window. Too many evenings I'd huddle in my room trying to ignore their shouting from the kitchen, willing them to stop, wanting to flee into the dark world outside. But they would continue and I'd go down to sit for hours in the kitchen with them, Steve on my left, Mom on my right, me in the third green plastic chair, the broken one that pinched your back and never fit that ridiculously small table. As long as I kept my brother from hurting my mother, I called it a success. As I escaped into the world as an animal rights activist and later to adventure, I kept returning, yanked back by my concern for my mom. I was glad for my messenger job, also for a Saturday job I took as a baiter on crab boats that worked the ocean outside the Golden Gate. These jobs kept me away until late most nights, but they didn't keep me safe.

One Sunday morning as I tried to do some laundry, Steve slammed his fist into my face and when I hit the floor, he clamped his long fingers around my throat. His weight crushed my shoulders and drove my knees into the linoleum. A strange calm came over me as I studied the bottom edge of the cabinet, that ugly grey paint nobody had thought to redo, and finally the speckle pattern of the linoleum fading to a blurred grey; my last sight. It would have been if my mother hadn't tackled him and thrown him into the washing machine as if she was twice, not half his size. We won a restraining order against him, though win is not the right word. Standing outside the palatial doors to the courtroom, waiting our turn, I can still feel that confusion, whether to hug him and sooth his fear, or stand tough, his victim; my mother, his other victim, only a hug away too. He was twenty-two and, crazy or not, it was time for him to try to make it in the world.

Standing over Fifi's frame, reading the sorrow-filled cards across from the wounded Pentagon, I imagined the families that had been shattered along with the impact of the plane. Their words hinted at a much different sort of family than I had known, all the more precious, all the more painful to lose.

The next morning I bicycled with my host through crisp winter sunshine along another route into downtown Washington. We were on our way to a full-day America Bikes board meeting to define the national bicycle agenda for the upcoming renewal of the transportation bill—a more official continuation of the dinner conversation the night before. We followed a different path near the Lincoln Memorial from the one I'd taken the night before. I followed her pedal strokes along the narrow, weaving path, enjoying the sights and tourists bundled against the November cold until she glided right, nearly to a stop, and then threaded her bike across a tiny bridge that led to a small island in a pond. On the other side of the bridge she stopped abruptly before the paved area dropped down a few stairs into a half circle of carved stone blocks. I had expected to ride down the few steps into that lower area to look at the writing on the blocks. But she was standing over her bike frame looking straight down at the pavement. I did the same and as my eyes focused closer in, I saw a carved granite tablet had been embedded into the pavement right in front of our bike tires. I leaned over my handlebar and read the slanting script:

And for the support of this Declaration,
with a firm reliance on the protection of divine Providence,
we mutually pledge to each other
our Lives,
our Fortunes
and our sacred Honor.

It was the last line of the Declaration of Independence (the stone blocks below represented each of the signers). I read and reread the words, marveling at the intensity of their camaraderie, their belief in honor, that they would give up their lives and everything they owned to ensure the success of their mutual endeavor.

It reminded me of the commitment I'd once known as a teenager in the animal rights movement, even a bit in the environmental movement. It reminded me most of one particular battle I'd joined too late—the campaign to save a river that was drowning behind a dam not far from Yosemite in the Sierra foothills.

I was staffing a booth for the Fund for Animals at an environmental conference in San Francisco, when my friend Laurie came rushing over.

"Come with me," she gasped, "I have to show you something.

They're drowning a river and no one has thought about the animals."

I followed her to the Friends of the River booth that was covered with leaflets and posters announcing the drowning of the Stanislaus River and their campaign to stop the rising water.

"Ask them," Laurie said to me, "ask them what they're planning to do about the animals that will be trapped when the hills turn to islands and then go under."

"Okay," I said as I turned to the three friendly young people behind the table, "what are you doing about the animals?"

"We aren't doing anything," the young woman said. "We never even considered that animals would drown."

I'd just turned fifteen, 1979, and was holding down the three jobs at the Fund for Animals, the Marin Humane Society, and the Marin Wildlife Center. The third one is what had excited Laurie. She knew I had the experience and connections to rescue those wild animals.

I founded the Stanislaus Wildlife Rescue Program with the help of my peers at the wildlife center. It was the first organization I had founded, so I was especially glad for their support. Some joined my board of directors to ensure that I could raise money and record expenses legally. The Friends of the River people were an enormous help too. They found me a ride up to the river and a place to stay where I could also store my borrowed canoe and cages—a communal property for Environmental Traveling Companions (ETC), a river company that served special populations. Not only was the ETC land a base camp for my rescue project, I never had trouble finding a river guide to paddle the canoe with me.

The first day I was there, I paddled with an ETC river guide near the towering face of the dam, maybe a quarter filled, mapping the islands in the reservoir, noting the smallest ones first. The next day, we slid the canoe through the tops of the brush on the smallest island until we finally hit ground. Animals scurried in all directions through the branches. Laurie was more right than even she had imagined.

Over the next four months, with the help of a different river guide each day, I scooped hundreds of exhausted and emaciated squirrels, rabbits, wood rats, mice, and rattlesnakes from branches above the water, set them gently into cages, and paddled them to shore. The rounded golden grassy, oak and shrub-spotted hills that spread away upstream of the dam were slowly isolated by the spreading water, lulling the animals to seek their crests rather than swim away. By the time we found them, they were too emaciated to swim. I learned to let the island go under to make their capture easier, but it meant our timing and mapping had to be perfect. By the time we arrived, the animals were weak and wet, water lapping at them as they clung to the bending, waterlogged branches. The wood rats were always in the tips of drowned, majestic oak trees. They'd climbed inch by inch for months. The best way to catch them was by their tails, which meant we had to shove them into the water with our paddles so they couldn't cling to the branches. They were so emaciated, by the time we'd turn the canoe around only the tips of their noses were above water, so we had to reach down to find their tails. We also moved birds' nests to shore and jumped back each time I emptied my mom's laundry bag full of rattlers. They never even rattled. Maybe they knew we'd come to help. I'd empty the bag of a dozen or more and they'd slide away in a dozen different directions.

While I was busy rescuing animals, Friends of the River continued their fight to stop the rising water. Every one of the lead activists gave their all, spending weeks on the road lobbying politicians and special interests, then holding rallies at the river to increase support. They had been at it for ten years by the time I came along. They'd lost a ballot campaign that could have stopped the dam when their opponents, supporters of the dam, twisted their campaign messages to: "Vote no to save the river." These manipulators justified it later by explaining that the river would be "saved" behind the dam. Had the ballot measure passed, no dam would have been built. By the time I entered the scene, the dam was built and choking the river.

In May that year, Friends of the River won an important

battle. Mark Dubois, one of their founders, had chained himself to a rock in a secret spot next to the river at the exact elevation where the reservoir would be half filled. If the water's rise could be stopped at that point, one of the last pristine limestone canyons in North America would be saved. That upper section of the river was also renowned for whitewater rafting. At the end of May, after weeks of searching for Mark, sometimes nearly tipping over my canoe as they sped past in their motor boats scanning the shores with binoculars, the Army Corps of Engineers called a truce. They stopped the filling at halfway and Mark's only confidant unlocked his chains. My animal-rescue job was finished, at least for that year.

Alexander, one of the leaders of Friends of the River, invited me to join them on a river trip down the Stanislaus on June 1st. It was a special trip for dignitaries, state senators, and even a few members of Congress. All I'd planned for that day was to pack up, so I gladly accepted. We covered the nine-mile stretch of river in a few hours, the boatmen rowing downstream between rapids in order to reach a planned rally at the takeout on time. Even with the rushed pace, I was hooked. I'd never even considered taking a boat *down* a river. Rivers were things you crossed. The closest I'd come were those creek walks in Mill Valley, but this was no creek walk. Our boat banged into boulders, slid over drops, was buried in waves, then shot free to float quietly through a green pool before the next roaring drop. Trees with rope swings hanging over, the silvery grey cliffs framing the sky. This was something I needed to do, a lot.

As we came around the last bend, dodging the rocks under the old Parrott's Ferry Bridge, I saw the crowd. Hundreds, perhaps more than a thousand people were milling about in the clearing next to the road. A stage had been set up on one side. As we touched shore, Alexander asked me if I'd like to speak about the animal rescue. After only a few speakers he called me up. I'd barely had time to dry off or even get nervous.

On stage I told about discovering the battle for the river and my experience that morning that had shown me why they were so passionate to save it. I described the fear in the faces of the animals, how some would start eating the grass as soon we prodded them from the cage. I told about being jerked around by the Fish and Game Department who had laughed at my first call requesting a permit before starting the rescue, taunting me that I was just a fifteen-year-old (stupid to have told them my age) who had been watching too much TV. On follow-up calls, they claimed I needed a permit to rescue the animals, but always had an excuse for not issuing one. When I explained the urgency, they blew me off. I finally stopped calling and rescued the animals anyway, gaining some press along the way. A week before that rally, after four months of rescuing animals, I received their permit in the mail and threw it away. The crowd cheered.

That summer I returned to learn the art of river guiding, which became my summer job for nearly twenty years. I'd traded my pink-cotton, sleep-over sleeping bag for an expedition-quality bag that cost me a week's pay from the humane society job. I slept each night in that bag, usually under the stars, on the ETC land. Getting on a river trip was easy from there. I simply had to be there to help load the truck and, as long as they had room on the boats, they'd let me come along, riding the top of the load down the steep Camp Nine road that barely sliced a wide enough ledge into the vertical limestone cliffs. The guides taught me how to load and then run the boats—both paddling and rowing—and soon brought me on as one of their guides. The next summer I was hired by a tourist company to run several California rivers, but returned to guide for ETC on the Stanislaus any chance I could.

Mornings at the put-in on the Stanislaus remain vivid to me— the sun sparkling on the rushing green water below those blue/grey cliffs as we pumped each boat and shoved it in, the chill of the air above the glinting current, the rustling of leaves over us mixing with the gurgling rush, the smell of wet rocks and life, and that anticipation of setting off, the motion changing from river to shore sweeping past.

That first summer, though I also found I could get onto most tourist trips if I promised to help, I usually went along on ETC trips, learning, on top of the river guiding skills, a hard lesson about treating everyone the same, no matter how twisted or disabled they seemed. That lesson was finally driven home by an ETC guide named Bob. Polio had shriveled Bob's right arm and his left leg, so he was particularly twisted. He was actually only half a guide because the other half was Dennis, a strong, Scandinavian sort who happened to be blind. Dennis rowed while Bob sat behind him shouting directions interlaced with profanities depending on the level of danger. You could hear them coming for miles.

That first summer, at a lunch stop on an ETC river-guide-training trip, I stood next to Bob as we formed a circle and everyone joined hands. To my horror, I realized I'd stood on Bob's right, his shriveled-arm side. I was still staring at it, limp and hanging, when Bob grabbed it with his left hand and flung it into my chest.

"Grab it," he said.

I wondered if anyone would notice if I ran into those boulders behind us.

"Grab it," he said again. "Then we need to talk after this Kumbaya session."

I finally reached down and took the dead-fish hand between as few fingers as possible. When the circle broke up, I started down to the boats, but Bob called me over to where he was sitting on a rock. I sat next to him as he lectured me on not judging people by their physical abilities. His rage softened as he realized I was listening and watching as he pointed to various people, some in wheelchairs, others making their way through the sand with crutches. Bob's lecture cured me so thoroughly that in later years I often caught myself prodding people into doing far more than they thought their disabilities would allow. I stopped seeing their disabilities.

Also that summer, I had joined the fight for the river, helping to organize rallies, tagging along on road trips to try to convince farmers in the San Joaquin Valley that the dam, the fourteenth on that small river, would never provide any water to them. I took part in hearings in Sacramento and countless strategy meetings at the Friends of the River office in San Francisco. The river had captured my heart so I devoted my time to save it. My peers felt the same and they'd been at it for ten years already. Like the founding fathers, we were joined by this endeavor and gave everything we had to its cause, moving as one, ready to jump when the campaign leaders called us to action.

I expected to find a similar spirit of trust and unity in Washington, D.C. with the national bicycle advocacy movement. We would save communities from speeding cars by reshaping them for bicycles. We would create options for people who could not afford a car or needed a healthier way to travel. We would reduce air pollution, quiet and beautify cities.

The America Bikes board meeting was held in a room in one of D.C.'s oldest buildings near the White House. My notes from that meeting are interlaced with descriptions of the high-ceilinged, dark-wood-paneled narrow room, the long table, antique vases, and the tall window at the end that had once illuminated meetings of our forefathers. In those notes, I also hinted at my expectation of camaraderie as we discussed the turns in national policy we would make together.

That November day, taking part in that board meeting, I believed we were forming a bond in the national bicycle advocacy movement similar to the bond known by our forefathers, and the bond I'd known in the animal rights movement and the campaign to save the Stanislaus River.

Instead, our energy over the ensuing months was spent crafting accusatory internal policies that detailed every possible misstep any of us could dream of and how to reprimand such behavior when it occurred. Discussions about the transportation bill rambled into confused and diffused proposals that never moved past their impulsive form. In the margins of my notebook, next to my notes and descriptions from that first board meeting, I wrote, less than half a year later in smaller, tighter letters that rather than a focused cause and camaraderie I had found only tedious distrust.

Even so, I returned.

3
Fear or Trust

Six months after that first meeting, in early May 2002, I was back in D.C. for another America Bikes board meeting. After the meeting, the woman from Colorado, the one who had had no interest in my story about Rebel, invited me for a drink in the restaurant/bar on the ground floor of the K Street office building where the meeting had been held. We sat on high stools at the bar and discussed various happenings in the bicycle movement. The high ceilings and front wall of windows let in the early evening light and pulled my thoughts to the streets and riding Fifi. But soon what she was saying drew me back in to our conversation.

She served on the board of the Thunderhead Alliance, the national coalition of local bike groups whose retreats I'd attended, so she knew how close it was to failing. The current executive director was hardly more than a kid with a fresh MBA in hand. They'd hired him as the organization began to flounder and he'd only let it slide farther toward failure. She was soon to take a lead role at America Bikes, a coalition like Thunderhead, but of *national* bike organizations, and told me she didn't want Thunderhead included unless they replaced him. She thought I would be good for the job. I nearly fell off my stool. The way she said it, she had it all worked out, that I would be a shoo-in. Though I was disheartened by the national level of the bike movement, Thunderhead was different. Thunderhead was supposed to support local bicycle organizations like Prescott Alternative Transportation (PAT), lots of them, all over the country. My job would bypass the national dysfunction and focus entirely on helping those local experts to transform their communities. I didn't give that young man another thought. The realization that I'd found my dream job wiped away any hint of empathy for him.

Back in Prescott, weeks passed without a word from Thunderhead. Then one day as my hope had all but faded and I was refocusing on my work for PAT, searching for a document in the file cabinet in our upstairs bedroom to finish a grant proposal, the phone rang. It was the board chair of Thunderhead, the odd one. I delivered my pitch, which I'd practiced with that woman in the D.C. bar, on why I was the best qualified for the job. I capped it with my offer to work for one dollar a month until I raised enough money to cover my salary. He hired me right there, over the phone.

As soon as I hung up, I slammed the file cabinet shut, skipped down the stairs, and began scribbling notes on countless scrap papers about Thunderhead's current programs and what the organization could become, all laid out on the rectangular wooden table against the windows across from our kitchen counter. I stared at the mission statement—creating, strengthening, and uniting state and local bicycle advocacy organizations—and noted ways Thunderhead could reach communities across North America. I thought of my own experience as the executive director of PAT, how difficult it had been to be accepted into Thunderhead, and scribbled furious notes on how to break that exclusive culture. The organization was in a tailspin. I would have to rely on the board's appreciation of my sacrifice in order for any of my proposals to move forward. Sure enough they approved them all at the next board meeting, held by conference call as I strode between kitchen counter and table, referring to my notes, soaking in their praise.

I had been working from home without an office space for years since much of my work for PAT and the bike shop was out in the community. Our house sits at the top of a steep dirt road that dead ends at the forest boundary with a clear view across Prescott and the grasslands all the way to the San Francisco Peaks nearly a hundred miles to the north. My husband Jim designed and built it with the help of his friends, including a wide deck facing the view. The north side of the house is dominated by glass—tall windows and double glass doors. While the house seems big with the large deck and open floor plan, it's not much larger than a small two-bedroom.

I studied every corner for the best spot for my new home office and landed on our music room to the right of the front door as you come in. It was packed with boxes of sheet music, records, audio equipment, and musical instruments. Even if we did have time to play, there wasn't any space. After getting the thumbs-up from Jim, I moved most of it to the basement, leaving my drum set in the corner and a few other instruments for décor. At a yard sale I bought a heavy, compact desk, handcrafted from oak and plywood sanded smooth and stained dark. I added a used office chair from a shop downtown and prepared myself to receive Thunderhead's computer and files. The short desk left just enough room for a two-drawer file cabinet on the left so I could leave the top drawer open and lean my left arm on the files. Shelves and a few cabinets along the walls completed the office.

Sitting in the chair at the desk, I liked the feel of it. I faced a bank of windows offering a view of piñon pines and junipers sloping down our hill. The soon-to-arrive monitor would block only a small square. Birds fluttered in and out of the trees and I'd never miss a coyote or bobcat sneaking past on our road. While I could swivel my chair to see the rest of the main floor, I felt sufficiently separated to expect to be left alone by Jim, our two dogs, and any visitors.

Those first four months volunteering my time as the executive director of the Thunderhead Alliance flew past in a whirlwind of frantic fundraising and membership development. The organization was nearly twenty thousand dollars in debt, which meant I had to do a lot of convincing for anyone to send us a check. There were only thirty-eight member organizations at that time, so I also reached out to potential new member organizations. I talked about the new goals and emphasized inclusiveness, networking, and the sharing of ideas. Because Thunderhead was a national organization and a member of America Bikes, I told potential bike-industry sponsors that we were creating powerful organizations that could influence Congress. I was tired of national power talk, but at least through Thunderhead it meant building organizations that were making an impact for bicycling.

Thunderhead's annual retreat was coming up in August in Minnesota, and next to nothing had been done to prepare for it. A bike advocate from Minnesota had reserved a Girl Scout camp. That's it. I'd spend half the day on the phone asking CEOs of bicycle companies for sponsorships and trying to entice more organizations to join, reserving the other half for planning the retreat. The scout camp had no staff and no bedding. We'd have to buy and cook all our own meals, three meals a day for nearly seventy hungry advocates. I took it on like a river trip, working with the Minnesota advocates to plan the food and bedding delivery.

For four months I worked on outreach, fundraising, and retreat preparation day and night and right through the weekends, never even saw those token four dollars. I had resigned as executive director of PAT soon after being hired by Thunderhead. I turned down parties and events, stopped playing tennis. Every minute I devoted to Thunderhead. I still owned the bike shop, leaving the work to my manager and mechanics, which meant I had some money, but not much, so Jim had to cover our bills. By the time I stepped onto the plane in late August to fly to Minneapolis-St. Paul, Thunderhead was out of debt and we had nearly twenty thousand dollars in the bank. The graph of our financials had flipped its mirror image into the positive.

I had arranged to stay with a local bike advocate in St. Paul that night before heading to the scout camp in the backwoods the next day. I took a bus from the airport to where he worked at a bicycle parts distributor. My plan was to stop in to see him, then go find a bike. Rebel in Denver nearly a year before had been my last Bike Hunt since all my other trips had been to D.C. riding Fifi. I was eager for my next Bike Hunt. But as the bus drove on along the overbuilt multi-lane swath of pavement out of the city and into long stretches of industrial lots, suburban sprawl, and dittoed fast-food joints, I began to realize this would not be an easy hunt.

After checking in with my host and taking a tour of the vast industrial building that housed the bike-parts distributor, I stepped outside into the glaring sun to gaze down that desert of pavement that disappeared without a bend in both directions. Each drawn-out block held only a few businesses, the gaps between filled with empty parking lots as if a lava flow of asphalt had buried the life of the place. If I were to start down that road in either direction expecting to find a business that could sell me a used bike, my hopes would be lost in that suburban wasteland. This was going to take focus and a lot of help from the locals. At that moment, in order to commit myself to that unlikely hunt, I devised two new Bike Hunt rules: First, once you decide you're on the Bike Hunt you must engage fully no matter how bleak it may seem. Second, the Bike Hunt starts by asking the first person you encounter where you can find a used bike. You must then follow their instructions to the end before asking another person, no matter how crazy they seem.

The Pizza Hut across the parking lot showed the closest signs of life even though lunchtime had passed. At the counter, I offered my dilemma to the young man who was pleased to help. He knew of a bike shop about ten blocks away (I stifled my gasp)—a right at the next side street, turn right at thus and so, then left after a block, then... I asked him to write it all down on a napkin.

The blocks were nearly as long through the neighborhoods, so I walked steadily under the weight of my backpack, at first enjoying the grand houses with their perfect paint, groomed gardens and lawns, the thick summer foliage of pruned trees, before the emptiness of the place quickened my steps. Well-kept people and places signified danger to me. This may have started with my father and his obsession with appearing rich, the delusion exposed through his violence. My apprehension was often confirmed living on the road, hitchhiking across this and other countries, usually in the fall between working as a river guide and winters as a bike messenger. The well-dressed guys in the fancy cars were the ones who gave me the most trouble. Even after recognizing this pattern, I had to force myself to break society's prejudice when I'd look into a mangled, rusted heap of a car, a dirty face atop dirtier clothes grinning back, beckoning me to get in. But ragged people rarely gave me a problem. In fact, they were more likely to buy me a meal. Many gave me knives, concerned about my safety. I'd stuff the knife into the bottom of my pack as a keepsake to remember them by rather than as a weapon.

Living on the road, when I'd stop for the night in a populated area, I sought out the ragged areas and their shadows—empty lots, under overpasses, bridges, stairways. People who would pass such places wouldn't bother me. Those shadows were my bedrooms, comfortable safe havens. I'd never sleep in a neighborhood like this because people who populate tidy, sterile places tend to fear ragged wanderers like me and fear can justify harm, as my father and brother had taught me. My father fearing failure saw the three of us as causing that failure. My brother, fearing life, saw me living.

I picked up my pace. Rounding the corner onto the last street named on the napkin I found the bike shop, a welcome contrast in its small pocket of life. A cluster of quainter, colorful houses plus a flower shop and cafe surrounded it, all shaded by lush, messy, unpruned trees. Most important of all, there were people. Was it the bike shop that had brought this life to this desert or had the bike shop come to this tiny oasis?

Alas, the bike shop had no used bikes. The owner was impressed by my story of the Bike Hunt, but warned me that my hopes of finding a bike in that area were slim to none. Fortunately, a customer had been eavesdropping and offered to drive me to another bike shop in the next town over. This made me ask which town I was in. The name was different from the town I had started in at the bike parts distributor. These "towns" had no seams.

After driving for many miles with this bike shop customer in the exact opposite direction from the place I was staying, I found myself at another bike shop that did not sell used bikes. I got another ride with another bike shop customer even farther out into the suburban stratosphere. By then it was nearly five o'clock and the likely closing time of the pawn shop where we were heading.

The driver maxed the speed of his tin-can import. We pulled up to the pawn shop just as a burly guy with a hardened face and messy dark hair was unlocking the cable that ran through a row of used bikes. After thanking my ride and pulling my backpack from his trunk, I turned to the pawn shop guy, doing my best to ratchet down the desperation in my voice.

"Can I take a look at your bikes before you put them away?"

"Sure," he said as he stepped back from them, obviously annoyed.

I balanced between feigned indifference and enough interest in the bikes to keep him from booting me out of his way. That gave me only a few minutes to find the best bike in the bunch. A bright yellow Giant Iguana mountain bike stood out, medium frame size, my size, with all his parts. I made sure to study the other dozen or so bikes, but he was the star. I pulled him out and began checking all his moving parts to ensure nothing was broken internally. Besides some loose bearings, nearly flat tires, and poorly adjusted brakes, everything checked out. The tires were evenly squishy so I knew there was no puncture, only normal air loss. I was holding the bike by the handlebar grip at arm's length to check for a bent fork and frame when the guy's voice broke my concentration.

"Do you want the bike or not?"

"How much?"

"Seventy-five."

"Seventy-five? That's crazy. The tires are flat, the brakes don't work, and it's all scratched up. How about forty?"

"No way."

I bided my time, returning to checking the frame and fork, but focusing past the bike on his adjusted stance. He had settled into the negotiation.

"Forty-five," I said, "but that's all I can do. I'm going to have to put a lot more money into this bike before I can ride it."

"Fifty, but that's my last offer," he said as he pulled the cable from the last bike and began coiling it. He had the knack.

"Okay, fifty, but you've got to throw in some tools I can use to fix it."

"I can do that."

I picked out a fist full of tools including an adjustable wrench, screwdrivers, pliers, and hex wrenches. After paying him and stuffing the tools into my backpack I set out walking back in the direction I had come from, rolling the bike at my side. We had to walk for five of those long suburban blocks before I caught sight of a gas station where I used the air hose and my new set of tools to make him rideable. But I found that his spokes were all messed up—some over tightened, others so loose I could wiggle them with my fingers. There was a chance that last bike shop was still open. I hopped on and pedaled hard, making it just in time. The owner seemed as pleased as I was that I'd found a bike and had no problem letting me use his wheel truing stand and spoke wrench. I bought a spoke wrench and bike map from him before setting out at dusk to pedal along the endless speedways.

At first I checked the map regularly, but soon learned that an inch on that map meant many more pedal strokes than I had anticipated. I stopped for a dish of spaghetti at the first locally owned restaurant I'd seen since leaving the bike shop, then pedaled on.

The turns from speedway to speedway were no problem, but near the end of the journey I had to find a hidden pedestrian bridge that led to the bike advocate's neighborhood. The bike shop owner had warned me that if I missed that bridge, I would have many more miles to pedal to the next river crossing. I found it, hidden mid-block, and pedaled onto it, the handrail width just enough for the handlebar to pass. There was no light along the bridge so I could not see its end. I slowed to glide carefully, straining to see the few feet ahead until the bridge ended. The bridge actually ended. I stood there, as high as the tops of the surrounding trees—mucky bog smells, night-bird calls, and insect buzzes all around—staring in the starlight at a railing at the end of the bridge. To my right the railing continued to the end. But to my left, there was a gap. I felt with my foot and found a stair.

Okay, there's a stairway, but maybe it only goes to the river. Maybe they've closed this bridge and there's no longer a way through. If I climb down to find nothing but river, I'll have to climb all the way back up, with the bike.

I glanced back into the dark, but remembered the bike shop owner's warning. It was after eleven o'clock at night and my host must have been terribly worried. I had to try the stairs. At the bottom, my feet landed on concrete. Could this be a bike path? Nope. It was just a square of concrete with dirt and grass in all directions. I chose one direction that seemed to continue the trajectory of the bridge, one careful step into the black at a time, rubbing through brush on each side until I hit a wall of impenetrable branches. I returned to the base of the stairs and set out in another direction, but my foot soon sank into mud. My third try found solid dirt and I continued, all the while knowing that I could be wandering into a forest labyrinth.

I heard the motor before I saw the headlights. The car rattled toward me on what appeared to be a rutted dirt road. I shot a glance back up to the bridge to see in that instant of light the direction it pointed. I knew from the map that I had to continue in the same direction as the bridge to reach the road I needed. I got my bearing just as the car disappeared and the veil of darkness dropped once again. The bridge pointed in the direction from which the car had come. With the visual of the dirt road imprinted on my memory, I threw my leg over the bike and pedaled into the black, into the ruts and over grass and back to the hard dirt as it sloped uphill. At the top of that dirt road where it met the neighborhood street, I patted the handlebar and dubbed him Grasshopper.

I doubt Bike Hunts like Grasshopper's would have been as enjoyable to most people. Escaping my brother to live on the road had given me an unusual perspective. The outside world was a safe and joyous playground compared to life at my mom's house. Even people who behaved strangely were not scary to me. Death seemed fine. I knew that standing on the side of the road with my thumb out could be an invitation for someone with a twisted vengeance waiting to be fulfilled. In fact, before I started any trip, before I'd let myself stick my thumb or sign out, I made myself say out loud, as loud as I could, "This is worth dying for." To face and accept death is to overcome fear. By alleviating my own fear,

I could settle in with and trust any person who picked me up, then focus on understanding their perspective, even if it included a fear of me.

I once caught a ride on a long stretch of desert road at dusk with a thin young man who seemed to live in three worlds. Our conversation for the next two hours was a loop that went like this:

"You're a hitchhiker," he'd say in a startled tone, "You're going to kill me."

"No, I'm not going to kill you," I'd say. "I just need a ride to the highway junction. I really appreciate you helping me out this way."

He'd smile and watch the road again. Then his expression would widen and he'd laugh as he said, "Jesus loves me you know. He's going to save me."

"I have no doubt that Jesus loves you. You seem like a really nice guy."

"Thank you." He'd hum a bit, eyes ahead. Then, "Shit!" he'd yell, "We're going to run out of gas!"

I'd lean over and say, "Nope, no worries, there's plenty of gas in the tank."

"You're a hitchhiker. You're going to kill me."

"No, I'm not going to kill you..." For two straight hours. When he let me out right where I wanted, he wished me safe travels. I was sorry for his fear of me. Something had taught him to fear hitchhikers as I had learned to fear wealthy neighborhoods.

I discovered my thumb the same summer I discovered river rafting, when I was fifteen and had finished rescuing animals on the Stanislaus River. Sometimes we'd have to hitchhike to get back to the truck where we'd left it at the start of a river trip. My fellow river guides taught me the basics—stand at the start of a pullout and never on a blind corner so drivers can see an easy way to pull over, stand near the road and look friendly, never sit or you'll look like you don't care if you get a ride.

My first long hitchhiking trip came at the end of a forty-five-day Grand Canyon river trip with a bunch of ETC river guides that capped that summer. On the first day of the trip, stepping onto one of the boats as we shoved off from shore, I asked someone on the boat what day it was. It also happened to be the first day of what would have been my sophomore year of high school. Over the next six weeks, we lived like lizards and fish in the crevices and pools of the canyon. When we got to the end of the river trip, our hippie-painted school bus wasn't there. The guy we'd paid to care for it and drive it to meet us had vanished along with the bus. There were eighteen of us so we broke into smaller groups to have a better chance of catching rides back to California, leaving one guy with the gear to figure out the puzzle.

That trip is when I realized that if all I needed to travel was a thumb, I could travel the world. The world map on the ceiling of my room at my mom's house came to life. I could go anywhere. I'd lie on my bed calculating likely hitchhiking times and how far I could go in the time I had. Escaping had taken on a new dimension, no longer a few hours out on my bike, but whole adventures across the globe.

Once I had thirty days between the end of the river season and my next trip to Europe. I had returned to Mill Valley to check on my mom, but soon regretted it as Steve hounded me. A friend from Prescott College was working as a guide in the bush of Alaska. I owed another friend in Prescott twenty dollars. With my finger, I traced San Francisco to Alaska, across Canada, down the east coast, across the states to Arizona, and back to San Francisco. I figured I could make it in a month. I left with my usual small pack and only that twenty dollar bill in my wallet. Made it back to Mill Valley with a day to spare and my debt paid, though I'd lost a bit of weight between free meals.

On that trip, dropping out of Canada into New Hampshire, a ride with a father and son reminded me that fear can sneak up on us. The father was in his seventies, his son only fourteen, the product of a late-life romance. They were traveling the Northeast, fishing and hiking, bonding. I sat in the back savoring their stories and easy banter, having to remind myself about their age difference as they were so close, so loving of each other. When they told me about fishing and their love of the outdoors, the kid describing some of their gear, I reached down in my pack to get one of the knives given to me early in the trip, this one from a Vietnam veteran. It was nearly the length of my forearm with a blade that curved to a sharp point, the upper edge serrated to rip guts. I drew it from its leather sheath to show the kid and describe how it may have been used during the war.

That evening, the father grew tired of driving and pulled over at a motel. He invited me to stay with them since they would continue south the next day. He got one room with two beds, he and his son sharing one.

I woke to screaming, shrill, terror-stricken screaming, and froze, searching the darkness for hints of where I was, who was screaming, and why. I remembered the kid, but heard his voice calming his father. A nightmare. To give them some space, I got up and used the bathroom. I left the bathroom light on as I came out, lingering at the doorway.

"Are you okay?" I asked.

"Yes, yes," the father said.

"You sure?"

"Yes," he said. "I'm fine."

I turned off the light and moved carefully to my bed. As I settled under the covers, I heard the father turn toward me.

"It was you," he said in a voice like he regretted speaking. "You were killing my son with that knife."

Trust is the opposite of fear, though it can switch to fear in an instant, as it had in this father's subconscious when I'd shown his son that knife. Fear is a trickster. Its source can be truth or deception like news stories that fixate on the unusual, fabricating a world where maniacs and terrorists swarm. Perhaps it reaches back to our ancestors who relied on fear to survive, when fearing the right animal or wandering foe meant the difference between life and death. Now, trust and fear are scrambled. We linger with the wrong people and fear those without threat. But as a young hitchhiker, I still had it right. I knew who to fear (my father and brother) and allowed anyone, no matter their appearance, to earn my trust.

On one of my early trips across the United States when I was still a teenager, my rides took me from San Francisco through the Central Valley and into Las Vegas. Dropped off at sunset on the north side near downtown, away from The Strip and casino glitz, I needed the freeway heading north in order to catch Interstate 70, but the spaghetti of onramps went in all directions. If I was going to catch a ride before dark, I needed cardboard to make a sign. The bleak streets had more vacant lots than occupied ones, chain link splattered with trash. The few low buildings I passed were locked down like reverse prisons, keeping the bad guys out. I checked the sides of buildings, crevices, behind abandoned cars, places where the wind had collected bulky trash, but couldn't find anything sturdy enough to make a sign.

Rounding a corner I found a sign of hope painted in bright red across a dirty flesh-colored flat-roofed building sitting between vacant lots: Bail Bonds open 24 hours. I had no idea what bail bonds were, but they were open and I was going in. The office spread nearly the entire space of the small building with only two doors on the far side that must have led to very small rooms, perhaps a bathroom and a separate office. A stained blue carpet did nothing to brighten the dull space, lit only by the dipping sun out the street-side windows. Two empty desks sat about as far away from each other as they could get, one under the windows to my right, the other at the back to my left. As my eyes adjusted to the dim, I searched for whoever was supposed to do this nonstop bail bond thing. A mammoth of a man moved out of the shadows on the far side of the room, shoulders as wide as one of the desks, shaggy hair and beard. As he moved toward me, the waning sunlight lit his curious smile.

"Hi," I said. "Glad you're open. I'm hitching toward I-70, but need a sign if I'm going to get through that mess of onramps out there. Do you by chance have a piece of cardboard you could spare?"

"Sure, little lady," he said, "I bet we can find you something that will work."

I wondered who "we" meant, but my scrutiny of the shadows

found no one else. "Thanks so much," I said and waited for him to go get my cardboard. But he didn't move, just stood there with that same curious smile.

"So, where you heading?"

"Cross the country."

"Where you live?"

"Nowhere at the moment."

"You hitchhike a lot?"

"Yeah." Okay, guy, time to go get that cardboard.

"How do you protect yourself?"

"From what?"

"From people who want to hurt you."

"Most rides are great, no intentions of hurting me," I said, realizing his smile had turned to a deeply worried frown. This guy expected a good answer. So I thought hard to remember any trouble I'd had from rides, a rare issue. "I guess I've had guys pick me up thinking they could mess with me, like maybe I was a road whore. No idea why, the way I make sure to dress." I glanced down at my patched army pants and baggy T-shirt. "But I just look them in the eyes and explain otherwise, tell them why I'm really on the road—to move, to live. They learn about me, then open up about themselves and soon that misunderstanding is forgotten. Only a few times they've pulled over and let me out when they realized they weren't going to get any." His concerned frown didn't change. I didn't know what else to say to persuade him to go get that cardboard.

"Do you carry a weapon?"

"No, why would I? I don't want to hurt anyone."

"Look," he said, getting agitated. "You've been lucky up until now. There are creeps out there who would hurt you so bad, even kill you. We're going to do something for you here."

He'd fixed on something and it had nothing to do with cardboard. I scowled at the darkening window as I realized I wouldn't be hitchhiking again that day. He went to the desk at the back, opened and slammed a few drawers until he found what he was looking for and came back to me with his hand outstretched.

"Take that," he said. "It's not much, but it's enough to protect you in most cases."

I reached out and took the small oblong object from his palm—a pocket knife with a carved bone grip, the metal tarnished from age. "Thanks," I said, turning it in my hand, another knife for my collection, thinking maybe that was all for extracurriculars and I could leave. But he snatched it back.

"Now, we're going to give you a lesson on how to kill with this," he said, and turned to yell at one of the doors, "Bill! Get out here!"

Bill appeared at the door, a smaller rounder version of the first man, beard and all. The big guy summarized why this blond teenager was standing in the middle of their office and his plan. They switched on the lights and shoved the desks farther apart to make as much room as possible for my killing lesson. For the next long hour I learned more about stabbing hearts and slicing arteries than I ever wanted to. The big guy started the lesson by showing me the long notch at the top of the blade that made it possible to open with one hand using my thumbnail. He made me open it over and over, faster and faster. Bill instilled the lesson of never showing that knife, or any other weapon, until I was going for the kill. If you wave it, they'll take it and use it on you.

Once I'd mastered opening it hidden behind me or in my pocket, the big guy demonstrated on Bill like he was my attacker. He showed how to hold the knife so the blade stuck up past my thumb for the best kill moves. He pretended he had the blade and swiftly jabbed it below Bill's sternum straight up to the heart and twisted. The twist, he said was the most important part. Next he showed how to move behind an attacker, stick the blade under one ear and slice fast and deep all the way to the other. The only time I should hold the knife blade down was if my best shot was a stab to the back, an unlikely kill.

Then I had to practice those two moves on Bill over and over again until the big guy was satisfied that I was a finely honed killing machine. At that point he went and got a piece of cardboard from out back, recommended I walk for about ten miles north past North Las Vegas and its local traffic, and they both bid me safe travels. After a few blocks, I stopped under a street lamp and took the knife out of my pocket to appreciate the concern of those two tough guys etched in its carved lines and that long thumbnail groove. Then I took off my pack and jammed the knife all the way to the bottom where I always put them. That long walk that night, through beaten neighborhoods, past more blocks of decay and trash, and eventually into the wild desert gave me time to slow my pace and contemplate the kindness of people, the kindness I'd tried to explain to the big guy, the kindness they showed me but could not believe existed beyond their stained office. After midnight, I reached my destination and slept a soft, untroubled sleep in a space between rocks at the foot of the interstate onramp.

Over the years, I hitchhiked across the states and around Europe so many times I lost count. Trips to Europe always included a hitch across country to either New York or Boston, where I'd catch a standby flight for about two hundred dollars, not worried about where, just the cheapest. While I was in Europe, I earned money as a street musician, playing a plastic flute (recorder) and juggling. On my third trip around Europe, I discovered the Swedish farm that became my true home, working as a farm hand and learning what family actually meant. Once I spent seven months hitchhiking around the world, though I had to fly the oceans when no ships took me up on my request to work for passage.

The freedom of the road was total. As soon as I set out on my own to hitchhike, I was free from the oppression of fear. Strange assailants were amusing compared to being confined with a relentless, known assailant. A switchblade dagger at my throat in the Paris subway was simply a strong message that I had chosen the wrong spot to do my street musician gig. Taken territory. No hard feelings, man, I'm moving. The truck driver who pulled a long-barrel .45 to shoot my black German Shepard, Meshab, when he pissed on his front tire was met with my block and a wrath of curses. Smiling at daggers and jumping in front of handguns is not normal, but it showed the level of freedom from fear I enjoyed.

I have a photo, clear in my mind, but lost in a box somewhere, of a spider-webbed windshield crack, sun casting rays from its edges. Past the crack, beyond the long nose of the black Freightliner semi-truck, the straight Nebraska highway extends to the horizon, rolling grassland all around. Ed is next to me driving, just out of the photo. Any other place he'd look right in a suit with a close shave and haircut, a grey gentleman. Ed is bemoaning what he calls buffalos—his name for the new breed of reckless young truck drivers. I empathize with him, noting I'd seen this in new river guides, even bike messengers who didn't respect the job. I want to snap the photo of Ed, to capture him for my yet-unknown future, but I know it would rupture his trust. So I snap the shot of the crack reflecting the sun, the day, and the memory of Ed. I'm happy.

Mornings on the road were particularly peaceful, awakening on my own patch of pasture or desert to the purr of the highway, invisible, free. Then to step onto the road, the conductor of my own ever-changing orchestra, and thrust out my thumb like a baton. Control without control. With that simple gesture, I was already trusting the person who would make that split-second decision to trust me, to turn their steering wheel and stop. There was music and dance in these maneuvers, the two of us plunging into the unknown. And why? Me, because it had become my life between the river season and working as a bike messenger. Them, perhaps to feel life again.

If the ride was long enough, our discussion could take that uncomfortable leap from the weather and small talk to their longing to be on the road, to be free. My heart ached whenever a ride made this turn. I heard innumerable stories of lives wasted because of commitments, because of children and hard family situations, because of jobs taken that never should have been taken.

The day after finding Grasshopper I drove with most of the Thunderhead board members in a borrowed van to the Girl Scout camp for our retreat. This would be my first appearance as Thunderhead's new executive director. The members were to arrive in the afternoon, leaving us little time to figure out what we were up against. I checked all the buildings of the deserted camp to figure out how it would accommodate our sixty-nine attendees. The bedding had arrived. The food was mostly purchased and waiting in the kitchen. Tables and chairs were neatly stacked in the spacious community room that doubled as the dining room. With a bit of help from board members and other early arrivals, we had it set to our liking in no time.

The retreat was an outstanding success. All the members I had invited to speak did an excellent job. Everyone pitched in for meals, setting up sessions, and cleaning up. There was so much energy flying around, I thought we could run a power plant. Not a hint of the exclusivity I'd experienced at previous retreats remained. I especially remember watching groups of Thunderhead members swirl together outside among the tall pine trees between sessions—sometimes two or as many as a dozen, hands exclaiming, hurried notes taken as they learned from each other. I'd walk by as nonchalantly as I could, trying to catch a word or two and enjoy the action.

Having that camp all to ourselves added to the intimate feel of those three days. We were in charge and could shift and mold it to our liking. From the interactive sessions to the laughter of meal preparations to playing in the lake next to the camp, the entire three days is a smooth brushstroke. That is, except for one disturbing moment.

It was the first day of the retreat. We'd circled up on the low wooden benches in a clearing between pine trees to introduce ourselves—from longtime Thunderhead board members to the newest members. The board chair was last to speak. He began with the heartbreaking story of one of the founders of Thunderhead. He too was a founder. The crack in his voice showed how close they had been. She had been killed that spring, two months before he'd hired me, run over by a bus as she was crossing a street on a consulting job for a bicycle project. We honored his request for some moments of silence before he invited others to tell their stories of her. I'd met her only a few times and appreciated their fond memories of her enthusiasm for communities made for bicycling and the advocates who created them.

That wasn't the moment that disturbed me. It came when the board chair broke the silence to point at me and declare that I had stepped up to lead Thunderhead, that everyone there needed to appreciate me and imagine what would happen if I died.

Time slows. All eyes turn to me, projecting my demise. I try to fathom the freakish replacement he expects me to be and the crash that must follow if I live instead. I gaze back at the other faces, appealing to them to know me for who I am.

I gave Grasshopper away on the morning I was to leave after the bicycle conference in St. Paul that had followed the retreat. During the conference, I had spotted a homeless shelter and pedaled right there in hopes of finding someone who needed a bike. The shelter was surrounded by a tall fence of steel slats with a locked gate. Lots of people were milling around in the yard inside the fence. A few lingered outside, mostly talking with each other, so not really candidates for Grasshopper. One very tall guy was sitting alone, but I didn't consider him because he was sitting next to a bike.

I rolled up to the fence and pressed my face against the bars to get a better look at the people inside, pondering how I would get their attention. I asked the tall guy how I could get in and he told me I probably couldn't. They wouldn't let him in because his ID had been stolen along with everything else he owned. No, the bike wasn't his. Now he had my full attention. When I gave him the giveaway spiel he gasped and stood, like a game-show contestant who had won the pot. When he swung his leg over Grasshopper, his wide grin blocking the morning sun, the bike looked like a toy. He assured me it wasn't too small. As I handed him the key to the lock, another guy with a knife-scarred scowl stepped forward. Before I could worry he stretched his torn face into a smile, thanking me for taking care of his friend.

The Bike Hunt had become my channel back to the boundless, tender world that I had discovered as a child. I had let this Thunderhead job constrict me, disconnect me from my friends in Prescott, the fun and activities that energized me. Returning to confinement and shutting out the world, I savored a taste like

Grasshopper's giveaway all the more. I could no longer thrust my thumb out into traffic and be swept away into fantastic adventures. I could not linger in roadside diners watching the road and wondering where it would take me that day, ordering eggs, hash browns, and toast from another harried waitress, sipping weak coffee with too much sugar from another of those battered, thick white mugs they all have, knowing freedom. Not thinking it. Not the exhilaration of newfound freedom. Just *being* totally free. That sweet taste of freedom in the smile of a scarred stranger's face.

Once back in Prescott, I focused on the requests our members had made at the retreat and ways I could make their work easier. I sought out or created from scratch model resources to post on our website—talking points for persuading officials to invest in bicycle infrastructure, sample press releases, and templates for budgets and grant proposals. I also realized we'd need more gatherings than the annual retreat in order to reach more bike groups around the country. I got to work on training curriculum and the board approved this addition.

We were on our way to end 2002 with seventy thousand dollars revenue, twenty-five thousand dollars in surplus to start 2003 off strong. We'd nearly doubled our membership from thirty-eight to seventy-one member organizations. Soon after the retreat, I asked the board for a raise from one dollar to one thousand dollars a month and they granted it. This fragile, newly revived entity still needed careful tending.

In October, I attended Interbike, the annual bike industry trade show in Las Vegas, as the executive director of the Thunderhead Alliance. I was so proud. This was my twelfth Interbike. All the others I had attended as the owner of Ironclad Bicycles. This time, I wore two hats. I found my longtime industry colleagues to give them a card and invite them to support Thunderhead.

At that time, all of the board members, save for the board chair, were eager to help me with planning our new trainings and choosing locations. They helped me develop the curriculum to guide leaders past common mistakes so they could focus their time and resources on increasing bicycling.

Since I still served on the America Bikes board, my schedule also included more trips to D.C. to attend their meetings. Each trip, I'd fit in as many meetings as I could with potential partners and supportive members of Congress. Days spent sprinting through the halls and tunnels of Capitol Hill, slipping on marble steps and brushing past massive marble columns with minutes to spare before the next meeting with a member of Congress, choking down dry sandwiches in the cafeterias as I scanned the faces for key representatives or senators or their aides, ready with the latest pitch, then lung-busting sprints on Fifi to meetings away from The Hill.

I learned how to pitch Thunderhead as necessary to achieving a great transportation bill for bicycling, whether in D.C., at conferences, or from my home office. When I would present a map of the country with our member organizations marked, obvious holes showed. I followed the lead of the board, claiming that we could build strong organizations in any Congressional district where a critical vote was needed. This brazen claim fell back on me to find bike advocates in the vacant areas of our country.

From my home office in Prescott I would start by searching the internet for any hint of bike advocacy in the chosen city. If I was lucky, I'd find an organization. Even a small one with a cheap website and a handful of volunteers was enough. Usually I found nothing, so I'd call bike shops. A bike shop that was active in bike advocacy was better than nothing. Some of these shop owners went on to found nonprofits. America Bikes had offered mini grants to help wispy groups like these stabilize so their constituents would contact Congress. As I made these calls, influencing Congress was secondary. Through this veneer of appeasing our national partners, I knew my work would help build great organizations that would shift their communities toward bikes. This political pressure simply helped me focus my efforts. Louisiana stuck out not only as a void for bike advocacy, but one of the top Congressional districts for influencing the transportation bill. Without that pressure, I never would have found Frank in New Orleans.

As far as I could tell, there was no bicycle advocacy organization serving New Orleans when I began my outreach to that city. I'd found a bike committee, a club, and some bike shops on the web and started calling. Each person who answered said they weren't the one to speak with, that I needed "Frank, the bike guy," but didn't have his number. After several calls, I changed my request to how I could find Frank, the bike guy.

On the third day of my city-wide phone volley, a mechanic at a French Quarter bike shop found the phone number of Frank's cousin. Frank's cousin then gave me the number of Frank's mother. I dialed Frank's mom expecting her to give me yet another number.

"Hello," I said when she answered, "I'm trying to find Frank because everyone says he's the best person to speak with about bicycle advocacy in New Or..."

"FRAAAAAANK!" she shouted half into the receiver as I held it from my ear.

"Yeahp," was the next thing I heard. It was Frank. I'd found him.

Frank was indeed the bike guy for New Orleans. He was heading up the committee and teaching bike riding and repair at a charter middle school. He wanted desperately to see a bicycle advocacy organization formed for his city. Music to my ears.

Over the ensuing months, Frank and I worked over the phone and through email, gathering potential founders. In the end, we both realized that a training was needed in order to drum up the necessary enthusiasm. There was no question about the date— April, the time of the Jazz Festival. Frank formed a ground team to help organize the three-day training and found us a sunlit, spacious room at the charter middle school where he taught his bike course, not far from downtown.

By then, I had finalized the rules of the Bike Hunt. I was especially looking forward to following the rule that discovery of the community is the main goal of the hunt. I'd only driven through New Orleans on that drive across the country with Boston Sue twenty years earlier so it remained a mysterious place of alligators and sequins, Southern charm and strange language until April 2003, on the Bike Hunt. I had the afternoon to find a bike since Frank wasn't expecting me until evening. As always, the hunt took the whole time. I had taken a bus to the neighborhood where Frank lived, northwest of downtown. His mom had passed away several months earlier, half a year after our fleeting phone conversation, so he was living at her house to get it ready to sell.

I got off the bus on the busy road outside his neighborhood and asked a gentle older woman where she thought I could find a used bike. She pointed across the street to a thrift store in a run-down strip mall at the back of a vast parking lot. I thanked her and headed that way. That thrift store had no bikes, but the woman at the counter directed me to the next block down where I'd find another thrift store. This was not the New Orleans I had envisioned. The multi-lane road sliced through strip mall after strip mall. But as I walked, I found hints that I was there. The road passed over muddy creeks that beckoned me to stop and check for alligators in the reeds and shallow water. I didn't find any, but I was sure they were hiding just out of sight.

Each strip mall had a thrift store, but all were lacking bikes, at least adult bikes. I wondered if this was because adults didn't ride bikes in this city or whether so many low-income adults rode that the thrift stores couldn't keep them in stock. In any case, I was striking out. After walking a few miles and searching through half a dozen thrift stores, reality settled in. I was going to be riding one of the kid's bikes I'd encountered. One had caught my eye in the second store—a sturdy boy's twenty-inch-wheeled BMX bike, repainted royal blue. I walked fast, my backpack swaying, to reach it before five o'clock. I arrived as a young woman was flipping the sign to closed. She let me in when I explained I knew exactly what I wanted.

He was still there, buried and tangled among pink and purple girls bikes with training wheels and flowered baskets. I imagined he was as pleased to see me as I was to see him. I pulled him free and checked him over. His coaster pedal-back brake worked fine and all his bearings were adjusted—ready to ride. I paid the nine dollars marked on his handlebar and wheeled him out the door.

Pedaling through the parking lot and onto the quiet tree-lined streets of the neighborhood where Frank lived, I kept catching my knees on the handlebar. I had to stand to pedal, but the crank arms for the pedals were so short, my legs didn't know how to make such small circles. I'd get a few strokes in and then hiccup, once nearly launching over the handlebar that sat right under my stomach. I'd coast and then give it another try. Three, then four pedal strokes, then six and ten, until I pedaled a full block without catching my knee. A massive, leafy tree arching over the street had buckled the sidewalk into a perfect ramp. I couldn't resist. I pedaled hard, shot onto the sidewalk by way of a driveway, then straightened out in time to lift hard on the handlebar and fly. Skidding sideways to a stop, I jumped off laughing, holding the little bike at arm's length to get the full view of him, and dubbed him Lewy. The name popped into my head, spelling and all. It had something to do with his state and musicians, misspelled because I didn't yet know his city.

Frank was in the backyard of the expansive, single-story house—a power pack of energy with an expressive face ringed in white hair and cropped beard. A few out-of-town bike advocates had already arrived and were helping Frank with the barbeque. By the next evening we had piled seventeen of us into that house, ready for the days spent at the training and the warm spring evenings back at that backyard where the advocacy discussions over street redesigns and enticing new bicyclists to ride continued into the night.

This house was also our basecamp from where Frank and his ground team operated. Frank had arranged the freshest food for our meals, beyond what most people consider fresh. This struck home the first morning of the training when I stepped outside to ride Lewy to the school a bit ahead of the others. Looking down and fumbling with my bag as I walked, I nearly collided with a tall, spindly man I'd met briefly the night before.

"Got yer fish," he said triumphantly as he pointed to a large cooler.

Fear or Trust | 77

"Huh?" was all I could think of for a response.

He flung the cooler lid open and inside, nestled among cube ice, were several each of at least six different types of fish. I gawked as he rattled off the names of each species and described his morning—up before dawn, alone in his little skiff way out in Lake Pontchartrain, even the different baits he'd used. Within hours, those fish had become a key ingredient of a delectable seafood gumbo lunch.

Besides fourteen bike advocates from other cities, two national bicycle advocates from Washington, D.C., and the three of us presenters, most of the more than forty training attendees were locals. These locals with their guarded expressions and folded arms stood out for me among the out-of-towners.

I had made sure the curriculum was as interactive as possible, guiding the other presenters to offer no more than ten minutes of one-sided info delivery before inviting discussion. No presentation on bicycle advocacy or nonprofit management could fit all the innumerable variations of local organizations. Each has its own culture, expertise, and passion that come not only from the founding and current leaders of the organization, but from the unique communities each serves. To make these trainings valuable for the local leaders, we had to adapt to their needs from the beginning.

The New Orleans training took off like a rocket, fueled by the enthusiasm of the out-of-towners. We debated bicycle facility designs, engaged in heated discussions over membership fees, and broke into small groups for peer review of program plans. As the energy popped around the brightly lit classroom, its soft yellow walls and pillars covered with art from the middle school students, I kept my eye on the locals. They were participating only by listening, their furrowed brows discontented, distrustful.

Frank and his cousin spent most of the time outside in the schoolyard cooking on three portable tables and several camp stoves, surrounded by stuffed coolers. Each had held jobs as master chefs. Just before lunch on the first day, I snuck outside to consult with Frank about the locals. Standing amidst wafts of eye watering peppers, seared chicken, and tangy vegetables, he laughed at my concern and eased my mind by explaining that New Orleans locals are always suspicious of outsiders. Not to worry, though. He'd been checking in with them and they were intrigued by the prospects of a bicycle advocacy organization for their city.

Back inside, I mingled among the small discussion groups and watched as the locals would lean in, then scribble quick notes to capture what they were learning. My mind eased and by the end of the day, I was content to see them capturing the training in their own, careful way.

So, the next day I was not prepared when a small group of these locals approached me. I was up front, shuffling papers as another presenter discussed budgets. The four of them stood in a half circle around me and waited until I looked up, giving them my complete attention.

"Sue," one of the young men said, "we need to ask you a question."

"Of course," I said, "what is it?"

"What is up with the men in black?" he asked and the others made supportive sounds.

"Men in black? What are you talking about?"

Rather than answering they all turned to look to the back of the room. I followed their eyes and stopped on the two national bicycle advocates who had pressed their chairs against the back wall, their legs stretched in front of them as they whispered in each other's ears. They were both in fact dressed from tip to toe in black. I hadn't noticed their disrespectful behavior and suspicious attire. These peers from the America Bikes board had blended into my new normal. The local New Orleans bike advocates showed me I had already spent too much time in Washington.

As soon as the budget presentation was over I asked these two men to stand and fully introduce themselves. To their credit, they joined the discussions and by the next day, even included a few more colors in their clothing choice.

After the training, after our final mass BBQ at Frank's, after riding that city's maze of streets canopied with trees dripping moss and dancing until I was dizzy at the Jazz Festival, I gave Lewy to

Frank's bicycle program at the middle school. Sometimes he had to turn students away from the program because they didn't have a bike. Lewy found a way to give back to his city as I returned to Prescott, to my dream job helping bike advocates transform their communities into delightful places where anyone could ride a bike, and to prepare for our next retreat, this time at the very place where the Thunderhead Alliance began.

4
Delusions

The Thunderhead Alliance got its name from the Thunderhead Ranch in Wyoming, not a typical namesake for a bike group. Then again, the forming of this group was not typical either. It began in 1996 when a different national organization decided that if they could bring together the leaders of the most influential local and state-level bicycle organizations, twelve at that time, they could control their messages to Congress. That year, 1996, was the start of the reauthorization of the first United States federal transportation bill that had ever included funding for bicycle provisions. This national organization was dead set on increasing that funding in the new bill. Along with other national bike and trail organizations, they insisted on the involvement of local bicycle organizations in order to influence key Congressional districts for the bill, a song that was replaying too loudly seven years later as I settled into my job at Thunderhead.

Back in the summer of 1996, that national organization worked with a Wyoming bicycle advocate to reserve the Thunderhead Ranch, a remote ranch one hundred miles east of Jackson where they were sure to hold the attention of attendees. The goal of the gathering was to show leaders of local bike groups how to deliver a coordinated message to Congress. While some of that took place, the unexpected outcome was that the twenty-five attendees were so excited to finally meet each other, they couldn't exchange stories fast enough. They learned how their peers had succeeded with campaigns and compared notes on strategies for improving bicycle provisions.

The next year, these local advocates organized their own retreat without the help of any national organization, returning to the Thunderhead Ranch. They focused their gathering on what had been most valuable to them the year before—sharing experiences from the local level. They formed their mission of creating, strengthening, and uniting state and local bicycle advocacy organizations and named this new coalition the Thunderhead Alliance.

This story of Thunderhead's formation captivated me and softened the sacrifices I'd made to revive it. Those founding members, some still on the board, often reminisced about that 1997 gathering and showed their pride in sidestepping the other national organizations that had never understood or cared about the unique needs of local advocates. So, as Thunderhead regained its feet after our wildly successful retreat in Minnesota, I had begun discussions with the board and others about how to take our 2003 retreat back to the ranch. I was sure this homecoming to the place of the organization's birth would give it a boost.

In 2003, much as in 1996, the national advocates were frantic over the chance to increase funding for bicycling through the next reauthorization of the transportation bill. As the final retreat planning came together and registration closed, nearly one quarter of the fifty-two registrants were representatives of various national organizations, attending to persuade our members to lobby Congress with their particular message—some emphasizing trails, others performance measures, others highway provisions, still others safe routes for school children.

These national advocates had begun pushing our members to lobby Congress well before the retreat. In their messages to our members, they expected to meet them at the retreat to discuss their plans, which could explain the low number of registrations from our members. Even four of the nine Thunderhead board members chose not to attend. Not a good sign. To my dismay, all board members, attending or not, also pushed this national agenda as the theme of the retreat and expected me to do the same, their earlier pride in snubbing the national organizations gone.

I heard more than my share of this at our strategic planning meeting the day before the retreat began. Representatives of one of the national organizations, the one that had first brought the Thunderhead leaders together at the ranch in 1996, had encouraged us to go through this strategic planning with them in attendance.

The meeting, held in a lavish room at a museum in Jackson, became a tug-of-war between serving our member organizations and proving Thunderhead's worth at the national level. I was glad to hear a few of the five board members in attendance join me on the side of serving our members. With four board members absent, though, the meeting was more strategic for the other organization than for Thunderhead. The Thunderhead board chair pushed for national influence and the few of us who favored our locally focused mission were outnumbered. The result was to add a new program called the 50/50 Project that required Thunderhead to create strong state-level organizations in all fifty states and local-level organizations in the fifty largest cities in the United States. It stank of the old exclusivity. We'd have to favor organizations that fit this 50/50 mold. Rather than fight this turning tide, I determined to find a way to adapt it to serve *all* of our member organizations.

That evening we drove together in a van to the legendary Thunderhead Ranch. I could hardly wait to see the place where the organization had started. Besides, I had worked on several farms and ranches around the world, so I was interested to see how the ranch operated.

In New Zealand, I had worked as a wool wrangler on a sheep shearing gang. Each day we traveled to a different sheep ranch on the east side of the north island that had hired our services for shearing their flock. Gang was the right term for us. We strode onto each ranch like raiders. On breaks, we'd flop onto straw bales or out in the ranch yard opening tall bottles of DB beer and passing around unfiltered cigarettes, no matter what time of day. We'd do the same after the last shorn sheep was pushed back out through the slot in the barn, our arms and faces slick with lanolin. When there was a lull in shearing, I worked on a dairy farm helping them bring in their hay crops.

I left the shearing gang to hitchhike all the way to the south of the south island along the east coast and back the other side. In New Zealand no one will pick you up if you are standing still. You have to be walking before they'll stop. One of my rides explained that people figure you're at least putting some effort in, so you're worthy of a ride. I had to walk past the best pullouts, but even so, they'd rather stop on a blind corner than pull over for an idler. This was opposite to the United States where I rarely got a ride if I was walking. I think Americans figure if you're walking, you'll get there eventually. I often walked for miles before I found a good pullout and only then, when I'd set my pack down and stood to face traffic would I get a ride. I walked many times in New Zealand, but never for very long. Lots of short rides and interesting people. Some gave me jobs on their farms and ranches. Or I'd just knock on doors to ask if they needed a farmhand for a few days.

A hitchhiking trip into Maine landed me a job as a blueberry raker. I'd wake each morning in the backwoods cabin to walk through the mist onto my row, my fellow rakers flanking me as we scooped through the low green bushes to fill our rakes and then boxes with the dusty blue gems, then collapse onto my cot at night with berries wavering across my eye lids.

On another hitchhiking trip, near the northern tip of Scotland, I worked for my room and board at the communal farm in Findhorn, known for their belief in fairies, which is why I'd gone. Supposedly, their ability to talk to the fairies that live in everything—from plants, to animals, to the soil, to their tools—had enabled them to grow award-winning crops on nothing but sand and rock. They knew the names of each of the fairies, even spoke to their garden tools like friends. By the end of my stay there, I decided that whether fairies existed or not, believing in them was a good choice. Their sincere respect for everything had resulted in the most immaculate farm I had ever encountered. Their vegetables were show pieces.

Then of course there was the farm in Sweden, Hillsta, my second home, or really my first, which I happened upon on a hitchhiking trip in 1983. I was heading north of the Arctic Circle to visit a friend. I'd carried with me a scrap of paper with the address of the farmer whom I'd met when he'd visited Prescott. I caught a ride to their village south of Stockholm, figuring I'd say hi and move on. I can still see the farmer's astonished face when he found me sitting with his mother at her round kitchen table, his ruffled brown hair and strong shoulders, hands on hips daring the apparition of me to be real, then his satisfied laugh as he sat down next to me and made me repeat my travel stories. They fed me lunch of herring and golf-ball-sized potatoes sprinkled with dill in that bright, messy kitchen that would become so familiar—the two walls of windows looking out to the fields sloping to the deep green forest, the red barns, the pond just below with ducks bobbing—then sent me out into those fields to work. No one had ever done that for me before—welcomed me not as a guest, but as a part of their family. After weeks enveloped in this new delight, a family who valued me and who I fell in love with through our daily toils together, I remembered my Arctic friend and embarked on an unforgettable hitchhiking adventure to see him in the dark of Swedish winter.

 I returned to that Swedish farm and my new family to live the life of a farm worker for six harvests over eleven years, running between tasks, driving a tractor one minute, picking and bundling carrots the next. Knut, the farmer and my surrogate brother, gave me the title of Chief of the Vegetables to oversee the daily picking and delivery of the vegetable orders. One of my proudest memories working at Hillsta was the first time I wore a hole through my wooden clogs. That takes a lot of running. I also worked for a short time at Knut's uncle's dairy farm, caring for the calves, helping feed the cows, and cleaning the winter stables. But the majority of my work in Sweden was at Hillsta always starting with the vegetables and, as the harvest ended and winter set in, sorting and bagging potatoes in the dusty potato barn, then delivering them to stores in the area.

 We arrived at the Thunderhead Ranch at dusk, set in a wide-open valley framed by low hills. Driving up the long dirt road lined by a split-rail fence, the tall grey barn in the distance, I could imagine it as a setting in any cowboy movie. The hosts of the ranch had a meal waiting for us, so by the time we were free to roam, it was dark. The hosts had given me and the five board members luxurious suites in a building near the cookhouse, not the bunkhouses beyond the barn where attendees would sleep. I was surprised to find such luxury on a ranch, but I knew that it was often used for seminars and retreats like ours. Our rooms, with their feather-stuffed bedding, fine western furniture, and private bathrooms, were designed for wealthy people.

After settling in, we gathered in a common room in the same building, poking around in cabinets, looking for board games or something interesting to do with the western items that adorned the corners. In similar situations with groups that had some time to kill, someone usually found something interesting to start a conversation or activity. But that didn't happen. We all eventually sat down in the ring of chairs and sofas, silently glancing around the room. On river trips when a lull like this happened, say dinner was over and everyone gathered around the campfire, even a joke could start a nighttime of antics and laughter. So I told a river-guide joke, something about a genie testing the intelligence of an engineer, a scientist, and a river guide by giving them each three metal balls with which they had to create something important. The river guide ends up losing one, breaking one, and leaving the third one on his boat. They didn't get it. I went to bed early.

The next morning, I woke at dawn to get a good start on the day ahead. Our members were due to arrive that afternoon. Before then, we had to fit in a short board meeting to recap the strategic planning meeting and prepare our plans for the two-and-a-half-day retreat. The night before, we had unloaded a tall stack of boxes that contained the retreat supplies I had sent from Prescott. I stepped out of my room into the cool morning, the sun not yet over the low hills, to stare in puzzlement at this stack of boxes and the football field of ground between them and the barn where they needed to be. The van had left. I considered waking some board members to help me carry them, but remembered the long list of tasks I'd already designated for each of them. In order to move the boxes alone, I'd need something with wheels. This was a ranch. It must have lots of wheeled contraptions lying around, maybe a wheelbarrow or a cart or a hand-wagon for moving bails.

I walked over to the barn, but discovered it was not a barn at all. On the outside, it was shaped like a barn, but the inside was set up for meetings. I couldn't even see pulleys or remnants of stalls that would show it had once been a barn. There was nothing in that building to help me with my dilemma. I scoured the bunkhouses and followed a creek to where I thought there might have been a pasture. But all the fields were fallow, so fallow they might have never grown a crop or even hay, had never fed a cow or steer. The place was empty, not one misplaced tool, forgotten glove, discarded grain sack, or anything that would show this was a ranch.

I returned to the stack of boxes no better off than when I'd started my search. Then I remembered the bike I'd found on my Bike Hunt the day I arrived in Jackson, the day before the strategic planning meeting.

She was a rusty, faded-pink girl's-frame mountain bike with small twenty-four inch wheels and ten gears. I had bought her for five dollars at a thrift store in Jackson and had to buy forty-five dollars' worth of tires and parts at a bike shop to make her work. She appeared to be a hunk of junk, but turned out to be smooth and agile. I named her Pearl, for her treasure hidden behind an ugly shell.

Pearl was leaning on her kickstand near the door to our sleeping quarters—no basket, no rear rack, those small wheels, tiny seat. I tried to imagine how I could move the boxes with her. Then I heard Mad Dog bark, "Do it and call me when you're clean."

The only time I ever complained about a delivery to Mad Dog, I regretted it. It was a similar situation, my first month as a bike messenger. I'd taken the elevator down to the computer storage room of some enormous company in downtown San Francisco. I asked one of the workers for the Sparkies pickup and he pointed to a stack of three huge boxes filled with computer printouts. This was 1981 when data was still printed on those arm-width, accordion pages with little holes running down each side.

"Yeah, Mad Dog," I said when he answered, "I think you gave me a truck tag."

"When I was riding," he yelled back, "I could carry five of those fucking boxes on my bike! Do you want the tag or not?"

I knew that yes was the only answer if I ever wanted another tag again. I placed one box into my extra-large front basket, then heaved the other two on top of that one. It was all I could do to keep the bike from flipping forward as I secured the bungee cords. Even if I stood on the pedals I wouldn't be able to see over them. After easing the bike and load into the street, I gingerly got on and pedaled, peeking around the wall of boxes, but mostly trusting that everyone would get out of my way. Somehow I made the three-block delivery and got to call Mad Dog back with a triumphant, "Clean!"

I wheeled Pearl over to the stack of boxes, then stood back to examine her. She was small enough that the distance between seat and handlebar was less than any of the boxes. Since the trip to the barn was a straight shot, I didn't have to turn the handlebar. I lifted a box and placed it over the seat and handlebar, then pushed Pearl to upright off her kickstand—perfect balance and easy to roll. I walked beside Pearl with each box perched this way, swooping back in a split second between loads, and had them all delivered in no time. Mad Dog would have been proud, even if he wouldn't show it.

The sessions led by Thunderhead members all exceeded my expectations. Several were led by national representatives and those fell flat. But as soon as a Thunderhead member stood to present, all eyes and ears locked on them. We were in the fake barn, its vast space allowing for a single circle of fifty-one chairs around the speaker. For one session on media promotions I had paired an advocate from New York City with one from San Francisco to show catchy messages and images with regular people going about their daily business on bikes and demanding fair treatment. Another session on campaigns was taught by an advocate from the state-level organization for Texas using her experience stopping a statewide bill that would have banned bicycling from thirty thousand miles of Texas roadways. She was a firecracker, not much taller than five feet, but delivered this story like a giant who had no trouble wrangling the whole state of Texas.

I was so proud of our members I could barely contain it. Not only were the session leaders doing a terrific job, those listening were riveted to every word and scribbling constant notes, jumping in to ask questions whenever they needed.

I'd felt a similar pride when I was working for Splore, a nonprofit in Utah that takes people with disabilities on outdoor adventures. I worked as one of their river guides for twelve summers, starting in 1980, their first year on their own. On spring training trips we taught our trainees how to raft and live in the wild, including how to invite our clients to assist using role playing with props such as wheelchairs, braces, and blindfolds.

On one such intense training trip, a five-day through Desolation Canyon on the Green River, one of us senior guides had a crazy thought: leave the trainees to learn from each other on the last day of the trip. We all loved the idea because we knew firsthand that you cannot truly learn these skills until you are responsible for your own boat and clients. There were nine of us senior guides, which was about the maximum number for the paddle boat we'd brought along. So, after breakfast and loading the eighteen-foot inflatable boats we announced to our twenty-four trainees that they were on their own. They were now in charge of all eight oar-powered boats. We'd see them at takeout.

On this trip, as with all Splore trips, some of the rookie guides had disabilities. Others had never been on a river trip before. Still others had never worked with a disabled person. For four days, they had listened to us and followed our lead. Suddenly, they were the guides and were responsible for the safe passage of people and boats from camp to takeout in swift water near the bottom of Swasey's Rapid.

As we paddled away, we prodded each other with gory details of mishaps that could happen including the worst, a boat that missed the takeout to be swept over the deadly diversion dam just below. Between these gory tales, the silences showed that I wasn't the only one with doubts about our decision.

On another Splore river trip the summer before, in Lodore Canyon also on the Green River, I'd watched a mother Merganser duck bob in an eddy with her six ducklings above a raging rapid that surged to the left and back again near its bottom. We had set up camp there on the right side of the river above the rapid. Everyone else was either on a hike or relaxing at their campsite. I stood at the water's edge to see what this mother duck was up to.

Pretty soon she quacked a few times. Her ducklings, six tiny balls of fluff, responded with identical quacks only much higher in pitch. Then Mom quacked a bit faster and they responded as they nervously paddled around her. Then Mom paddled away from them right into the current, quacking loud, as fast as she paddled, and they raced after her also quacking in their tiny voices. I knew there was a terrible, crashing hole on the inside of the bend and watched with horror knowing that if any of the babies didn't make the cut, didn't keep paddling as hard as they could all the way across the river, they'd drop into that hole and likely not emerge alive. The line of seven sliced across the current and dropped one by one into the small eddy on the left. Safe. Then, without giving them even a moment to relax, Mom began her quacking again and shot out of that eddy into the turbulent whitewater with her fluffy babies right behind. They pulled off a perfect run splitting between holes and sailing over the peaks of the waves. Whitewater school for Mergansers.

We paddled our boat to shore at the takeout and pulled it up, glancing upstream as nonchalantly as we could. We washed the boat, bundled the paddles, and stacked our miscellaneous items avoiding any mention of what ifs. When we finally saw the first boat round the bend of the rocky, foaming rapid we cheered, running in unison to the shoreline to welcome them in. The danger wasn't over and we all knew it. The thought of even one of them missing the takeout and dropping over the deadly diversion dam made my stomach reel. Between our cheers we interjected the occasional shout to row a bit harder, keep that angle, don't let that downstream oar drop too far into the water. They all made it. Our magnificent ducklings.

Sitting in that fake barn at the Thunderhead Ranch I began to think of our members as my ducklings. I would be their mother duck and offer any guidance I could to help them navigate away from danger.

With far fewer leaders of member organizations at this retreat than the year before, I missed the energy between sessions. I saw the occasional small group form to share ideas, but none of the clamor and urgency to connect that I'd witnessed in Minnesota. A bike ride was organized and led by the board chair for the solemn task of spreading some ashes of the woman who had died the year before. I started off with the group, but soon found that the ride was too competitive for me. I turned back with several other members who also couldn't keep up. Sometimes a Frisbee would sail by and I enjoyed the spontaneous play, but only a few would join in.

Another extracurricular activity that likely contributed to the dampened spirit was the constant drone of the representatives of the national organizations. They had set up their own work station in an upstairs corner of the barn with computers and survey sheets for questioning our members. They would call them up one by one to grill them about their region of the country, their budget numbers, staff number, how many paying members they had, and of course, what they could do to mobilize their members to influence Congress.

I knew how offensive these interrogations were to our members. Such numbers had zero correlation to the effectiveness of their organizations. The best advocates could cause significant change with little if any resources, just effective strategy and an ability to organize the right people at the right time. Many of our new members were proud leaders of infant organizations who had already won major victories for bicycle projects and policies. Yet their answers to the national representatives made them seem small and inconsequential. So wrong and so offensive. In fact, many large, well-established organizations cause little if any change, spending all their time maintaining the very numbers the national representatives were requesting. In my mind, the only point of interest from such membership, budget, and staff numbers was that large numbers helped the organization withstand setbacks. Unfortunately, this also meant that they could accomplish nothing, or worse, cause harm, and still survive. Because the national surveys only used these numbers, they judged large organizations as superior to small—a misguided and demeaning process.

I was relieved when the last retreat session was over and we could finally pack the boxes to leave that sham of a ranch. I had allowed the national nonsense, even helped those national representatives set up their parasitic station, so I could not scold anyone or point any fingers without pointing right back at myself. There was a danger in this misuse of our members and I could not see a way around it.

I had organized an extra few days of exploring with an advocate on the other side of the Grand Tetons in Driggs, Idaho. Only three retreat attendees signed up. I slept most of the first day there while the others went on a bike ride. I woke in the late afternoon, still groggy. I couldn't remember ever being that exhausted. We spent most of the next day riding bikes along a mountain trail through a national park and swimming in the rippling creek beside the trail. On the way out of town as we headed back to Jackson and our flights home, we stopped at a family shelter in Driggs to see if Pearl might find a welcome home there.

Our local host went in to explain as we waited near the van with Pearl. Within minutes, a woman in a flowered cotton dress rushed out the front door of the low building and headed straight toward us.

"Are you sure you can give us this wonderful bike?" she asked.

I glanced around to make sure there wasn't another bike sitting nearby. This was homely Pearl after all. I knew she was wonderful, but I didn't expect anyone else to make this judgment at first sight. But she'd already touched Pearl's handlebar and was ogling her up and down.

"Of course," I said. "We'd be glad if she could go to someone who needs her."

"You have no idea," she said. "In fact, I'm going to have quite a headache deciding which of our young women is going to get this bike. Maybe we could run a contest." With that her attention shifted entirely to Pearl.

"Well," I said, "she's all yours. And thanks so much for finding her a great home."

Pearl found her place where people appreciated her true value.

Back in Prescott, I continued my breakneck pace, starting each day, including weekends, dealing with at least three hundred emails, talking and emailing with leaders of member organizations, finishing administrative tasks, then finally working on our new programs until bedtime. Before then, all Thunderhead had really done was bring its members together either at the retreats or via our email listserv. The new trainings and resources I was developing were attracting lots of enthusiastic attention.

In the background, the constant demands from the national level to prove the worth of our member organizations continued. On Thunderhead board conference calls I heard the same. They wanted to know how I was reaching into the states and major cities identified in the new 50/50 Project as not yet served by a bicycle organization or only served by one they judged as inferior. Some of our bike industry partners had also begun demanding 50/50 results before they would renew their support of Thunderhead. I assured them I was in the midst of the outreach.

Much like my success finding Frank in New Orleans, this detective work often led me to strong advocates who I knew could eventually grow great organizations. But the 50/50 Project required not only connecting with them, but taking a snapshot of their current status. In order to satisfy my board and our national partners, I couldn't just say I'd found bike advocates who wanted to build an organization. I had to bring back numbers and dates for meetings with members of Congress.

I would start these calls with advocates learning about their achievements, savoring their details on hard battles won for bicycle improvements. Then at some point I would have to break in and ask them their numbers of members and staff, their budget, and how they planned to meet with their members of Congress. The change in their tone from enthusiasm to cold, brief answers always stung like a physical severing of our previous connection. I knew as well as they did that those meaningless numbers were all that mattered to the national organizations, that their true accomplishments would be ignored.

I was especially dismayed at how willingly Thunderhead board members supported the cold and offensive survey demands of the national organizations. All were leaders of unique state or local bicycle organizations like our members, so they should have known how offensive it was to judge an organization by blanket survey questions. I went along with them, which means I too was warping, though I clung to an ember of mother-duck concern as I sought ways to remold these national demands to benefit our members.

In the meantime, our members continued their work to change their cities and states into better places for bicycling. Most had met each other by then and could easily share their stories. Talking with these members and watching the listserv, I began to see patterns in the campaigns that succeeded. I realized that if we could develop general campaign planning guidelines, we could give our members the means to cause significant change. Then I could point to these guidelines as our means of implementing the 50/50 Project, add campaign successes to the surveys, and thus soften the offense of those interviews.

Of course, I wasn't the first to think of this. I began researching other movements that had defined campaign guidelines. Some emerged during the Great Depression. Saul Alinsky and his community organizing efforts that began in the 1930s stood out because he was the first to bother writing down the steps they'd taken to win.

The community development movement also captivated me because it relies on local organizations. These organizations bring neighbors together to demand housing improvements, parks, community gardens, playgrounds, and other amenities to brighten their neighborhoods and fight crime. I saw a lot of similarities between these organizations and Thunderhead member organizations. I joined two of their associations and registered to attend their events.

I found other insights in classic models such as the civil rights movement and Martin Luther King Jr.'s writings, Gandhi's quiet yet powerful style, and Abraham Lincoln's laser focus on long-term success.

I made sure to note my own experiences with campaigns. I knew all too well why Saul Alinsky emphasized drawing many people together around a clear solution to a problem. Then a group could expect their city officials to respond. But go to officials as an individual with one complaint or as a group that has no clear message, and it's all a waste of time. Complaining can salve frustrations, but it never changes anything.

Early in PAT's second year, I had gathered some of our more than one hundred paying members to study maps. We were looking for the worst barriers for bicyclists and pedestrians and quickly zeroed in on a high-speed road that slices between the west and east sides of town. That road prevented safe travel across our town unless you were in a car. Following its length along the map, we found an overpass that spanned a creek through a park. We rode our bikes there and identified the crossing of that creek, under that overpass, as our number-one priority for reconnecting our town, like a plug we could pull to open a flood of riders. We knew our problem all too well and had found a clear solution where we could focus our efforts. Had I gone to the City of Prescott with a request for my own personal bridge over the creek, I would have been laughed out of the room. Instead, I walked into the department head's office as the executive director of Prescott Alternative Transportation, an organization to be reckoned with.

I laid the map on his desk and explained why a bridge over the creek, under the overpass, was vital. It would provide a safe way across the high speed road, reconnecting the two halves of our town for people not in cars. He said a bridge there could only be built over his dead body. I reminded him that PAT had a substantial membership that could be organized around this. He dared me. I glanced back at the map considering my next move and found it there.

"Okay," I said. "You do realize that we are moving ahead with the bike lanes and bike routes on either side of where this bridge should be."

"Fine by me," he said, already looking back at the scattered papers on his desk.

"And we are soon to publish our first bike route map that will show these routes ending at this barrier."

"Sure. Whatever."

"And," I said, as I picked up the map and turned to leave the room, "I plan to let everyone know that you alone are the reason there is not a creek crossing there."

"Wait," he said, as I reached for the doorknob. "Bring that map back here." I laid it in front of him and he started poking the crossing spot with the eraser of his pencil. "I suppose I wouldn't be opposed to a small bridge there as long as you and your group come up with the money to pay for it."

With that go-ahead, I reached out to PAT's members as well as other partner organizations who wanted a trail and bridge there. Even the City of Prescott joined the action, assigning one of their staff to oversee the building of the first phase of the Prescott Greenways Trail through the park, all built by volunteers with donated materials and funding. They never knew that one of their department heads had tried to block the project. We ended up talking the Eagle Scouts into building that contested bridge as a donation and, after two decades, that bridge still provides stress-free passage for over four hundred bicyclists and pedestrians crossing Prescott every day.

My first campaign took a lot less organizing and time. I was twelve years old, my first year as an official volunteer for the Marin County Humane Society. They had called a press conference to discuss a controversial turkey race that was scheduled to take place a few weeks from then as a Thanksgiving publicity stunt for some twisted company. This company planned to rent live turkeys to whoever wanted to take part, as many as they could rent, then shout and scream at the poor birds until at least one crossed the finish line. The race had already gained lots of publicity, but the humane society wanted the press to note the inhumane treatment of the birds.

I sat in one of the lined-up folding chairs that filled the front room at the humane society listening to this horrific plan from the organizers. Silently raging below the photos of rescued dogs and cats, watching through the floor-to-ceiling windows as new owners skipped to their cars with their new best friends, hearing the cries of the animals on the other side of the wall, the whole presentation made me sick. I could not accept traumatizing any animal for commercial gain. Even worse, the representatives of the humane society weren't trying to stop the race. They simply wanted their side of the story included.

This wasn't my normal workday. I had been playing in a tennis tournament earlier that day and had taken a bus as soon as I was done in order to attend the press conference. I'd never spoken in public before, but my rage got the better of me. I gripped the head of my racket with white-knuckled fists as I stood. They hadn't asked for input from the audience, but I stood anyway.

"Why don't we just stop the race?" I asked through gritted teeth.

The room exploded in applause. When the press conference was over, I was surrounded by reporters asking how I planned to stop the race. I adlibbed as best I could. When I finally escaped the reporters, I found the humane society administrators and asked how I could help stop the race. They were thrilled that I had been bolder than them and made me their spokesperson for the campaign. Over the next week I answered countless calls from reporters and supporters. The paper ran a few stories on my impromptu campaign to stop the race. By the end of the week, the race was cancelled. If only every campaign for positive change could be that easy.

As I captured the essence of these campaigns in my notes, the turkey race campaign gave me pause. The humane society administrators had justified allowing the race as long as their opposition was noted. It's one thing when an overworked bureaucrat blocks a new project. Call it self-preservation, protecting the status quo that ensures he leaves work in time for dinner. It's quite another thing when the advocacy organization charged with serving and protecting their constituents allows abuse to continue. I was allowing the national organizations to hijack our members and my opposition to this was too easily quelled.

Another campaign and another ranch haunted my thoughts as I worked. Friends of the River had launched the campaign to save the Stanislaus River ten years before I came on the scene to rescue the wild animals, so I didn't know much of the particulars when I started. I knew that the dam was built in spite of their campaign. I had also heard the horror stories about their ballot measure, which would have prevented the dam, but was defeated by lies that confused voters. As I spent time around the river, I met many river guides who had voted against it after hearing or seeing the opposition's propaganda using "save the river, vote no" as their consistent message. There was so much energy, so many people all over California fighting that dam and yet one heavily funded, deceitful opposition campaign was all it took to knock them down. They got back up and even stopped the water rising for nearly a year at the halfway point with Mark Dubois' bold move to chain himself to the rock in 1979, soon after I had started my wildlife rescue. But the river was drowned anyway.

This likely end to the campaign struck home one night during my second spring there. I had finished rescuing animals for the day and had stashed my canoe so I could meet up with some river advocates near a bridge that was soon to go under. They were planning to walk upstream to the encampment that had followed the line between river and reservoir since the gates had shut on the dam. I had joined this vigil several times, but never arriving at dark. We set off along the edge of the reservoir, twilight still lighting our way, but had to follow it way back away from the old river bed because the side stream was now a wide arm of the dead water. Up that side stream I knew there was a ranch that had raised cattle in the area for at least three generations. I hadn't even considered what would happen to them. I had been focused on the animals that lived there, not the people. I smelled the smoke before I saw the flames. We climbed over a hillock to the shock of a raging fire. One of the advocates knew the story. The ranch house, barn, and outbuildings had been set aflame so that motorboats wouldn't get their props hung up on their roofs. I couldn't move. Instead of walls and windows and roofs collapsing into the flames, I saw those three generations burning, that family who had built that place and worked it with pride.

The others had gone ahead, so I could see their dark silhouettes against the flames, like mourners at a funeral pyre. Darkness pressed in from all sides and a cold wind had begun to blow, whipping the flames. I saw hands reach out to the warmth. Reluctantly, I joined them, warming my hands in our solemn silence before following the water's edge back toward the river. That dead arm of water would drown the coals of the ranch in a few days.

I continued to help with the campaign through that summer and winter. The next spring of 1981, the gates of the dam slammed shut again, and I was back to my job of rescuing animals. The water rose above Parrott's Ferry and by summer when the spring runoff slowed and the reservoir stopped rising, I could no longer stand to go on river trips to end in that cesspool of scum and floating garbage. I knew there was no stopping the dam operators anymore, that the campaign had failed. Fortunately, I'd found my job with Splore and new river adventures in Utah and Grand Canyon, jobs I continued each summer into the late nineties. I ran away from the Stanislaus, campaigns, and advocacy. I couldn't bear the heartbreak of knowing those gentle green pools above the rapids, the rope swings, the diving pools up side streams, the caves in those silvery cliffs, that ancient fig tree by the river's edge, would all be drowned in that scum.

I found joy in guiding disabled people down rivers, hitchhiking the world, riding as a bike messenger. But even as I'd settled in Prescott running my bike shop, playing tennis once again, and enjoying my friends, I'd felt a void until I founded PAT. The successes of our early campaigns had rebuilt my courage for activism and led me to my job at Thunderhead.

As I sketched my notes on campaign steps, I was determined to make them so excellent, so easy to follow into success, that none of our members would ever have to experience the heartbreak I'd suffered as the Stanislaus drowned. I would show them how to stand up against anyone blocking great bike projects or using deception to stop their important work.

5
Bully

By late summer 2003, I seemed to have found a rhythm of satisfying the board and national organizations even as I worked on the campaign guidelines for our members. Our upcoming fundraising gala in San Francisco in November would showcase the work of our member organizations to bike industry representatives and Thunderhead supporters. And another trip meant another, much needed Bike Hunt.

Settling in at my home office in Prescott for this two-month stretch until that event, I was blindsided by the board chair.

When the phone rang, I expected one of our members. I often scheduled special meetings with leaders of our member organizations to help them work through their unique situations, but had none scheduled for that afternoon. Sometimes an unexpected call from a member could mean an emergency on their end, an organization crisis needing my full attention to guide them away from panic. Instead, I was the one who panicked.

Without even saying hello, the board chair hissed in monotone that he would resign from the board if I didn't format the work plan the way he wanted. I rose out of my chair, heart pounding as I asked careful questions. It wasn't the content of the work plan he was concerned about, just the formatting. I couldn't comprehend what he was saying and so stalled by asking more questions as I paced in front of our glass front door vaguely noticing the darkening clouds forming over Prescott and the central Arizona grasslands beyond on that sultry August afternoon. Nothing clarified. He referred to a draft of the work plan we'd started at the strategic planning meeting, but I could not decipher his problem with it, a problem so profound that, if not resolved, he would resign after eight years on a board he'd helped to found.

I knew I had to prevent his resignation because, even though the organization was finally stabilizing, such a melodramatic exit by one of the organization's most prominent figures would rattle its shaky foundation. I was quite sure he understood this too, but I couldn't fathom his motive.

The conversation only got weirder. I asked for details on how I could adjust the format and he told me I wasn't listening. I allowed him some silence, hoping he'd fill it. He fell silent as well. I offered different types of formats and he screamed back that I had no idea how to format a work plan. This had nothing to do with the work plan. Heavy raindrops plopped onto our deck, lightning flashed, thunder shook the house, and the rain turned to torrents. I realized the only thing that would prevent him from resigning was a great sacrifice from me. I offered to fly to Chicago where he lived, to sit down face-to-face with him to work out a solution (for what, I hadn't a clue). He accepted and hung up. I bought the expensive last-minute ticket with my own money, set aside my work, cancelled my meetings, and flew to Chicago.

I needed this Bike Hunt more than any before it, for my sanity, for reconnection to the real world. I had two hours after landing to find a bicycle before I had to meet him. After checking in at the hostel near Loyola University on the north side of the city, I had one hour left. I started with the wrestler-shaped desk clerk who helped me rifle through tomes of yellow pages on the glass counter that displayed Chicago memorabilia. Frustrated, he shoved the books to the side.

"Look," he said, "your best bet is to take this road right out here, take the first left and follow that street until you're on the other side of Broadway. There's a block of thrift stores along there and one's got to have a bike for you."

I thanked him and took off running. I'd brought my small

backpack with the papers I'd need for the meeting since I was sure I wouldn't have time to return to the hostel. It bounced on my back as I focused on planting each foot as far and as fast as I could. The first thrift store was overflowing with antiques, no room for bicycles. I backed out of the door without asking and shot a glance down the two-lane street for the next. The sign over the sidewalk had both the words "thrift" and "antique." My hope sank as I realized the desk clerk had sent me to antique row, no place to find a bike. But I forced myself to stick to the Bike Hunt rule that required me to follow his directions to the end until I had checked every one of the shops along this block.

As soon as I recommitted to the hunt, I saw the wheel. It protruded ever so slightly from behind a lamppost in front of that next shop. I ran straight to it. He was a knockout. Beach cruiser frame, wide chrome handlebar, flat black paint, whitewall balloon tires and five gears. I moved him as far away from the lamp post as the chain allowed. What a lunker. He must have weighed fifty pounds. Even his spokes were heavy-duty, twice the thickness of common spokes.

The shopkeeper came out, stated forty-five bucks. I offered forty, holding out two twenties and he took them with his right hand as he reached for the key with his left. The bike checked out fine, but needed air. I also wanted to make sure the axle nuts were tight so the wheels wouldn't fall off. I rode him slow along the sidewalk to keep from pinching the tubes. At the next intersection I found a Jiffy Lube and rode into the empty bay. A small, friendly Latino man greeted me.

"You need an oil change?" he joked

"Nah, I think his oil's good, but I do need some air." I watched him reach for the air hose before I dared the touchy question. "I also need to borrow some tools to make sure everything's tight." He stopped, air hose in hand. "Just a fifteen millimeter open end wrench and a six millimeter Allen if you have them."

"Yeah, I've got them," he said, "but if my boss catches me letting you use them, I'll lose my job."

"I'll be really quick and take all the blame if he catches us,"

I said.

He handed me the air hose and went to his tall red toolbox as I flung my backpack to the floor, aired the tires, and got ready to wrench. I used the fifteen first to tighten the axle nuts—good thing, they were all loose—then used the hex Allen wrench to tighten the stem and handlebar bolts—also all loose. I had my head down, putting all my weight into the wrench, when I heard the mechanic's urgent whisper that his boss was coming. I shoved the wrenches into his palm, thanked him and rode out the other side of the bay and onto the street thrusting the bike forward, playing with the grip of the wide tires and the tractor-like steering of that crazy, wide handlebar. The balloon tires absorbed even the deepest potholes. I tried hopping a curb like I used to when I rode cruiser-type bikes as a bike messenger, but the rear tire hit. This bike was much heavier than any of the messenger bikes I rode.

What luck, I thought, as I powered back onto the street, to have found such a great bike with such little time. The meeting was still half an hour away.

Shit! The meeting! My backpack with all the papers. I slammed on the brakes, laying down a long skid as I forced the bike around and back toward where I'd come. A delivery truck swerved to miss me as I pushed the pedals hard to get the bulky bike up to speed, riding against traffic until I found a gap to cross into the lane going my way. How many blocks had I dallied? Pedaling as hard as I could, my lungs burning, I searched the distance for that red Jiffy Lube sign. Finally I saw it, leaned across the lanes and into the bay. My backpack lay where I'd flung it. The nice mechanic came out of the glass-enclosed office as I lifted it to my shoulder.

"I knew you'd be back," he said. "I was keeping my eye on it for you."

"Thank you," I said, still catching my breath. "Thanks for everything."

He nodded and smiled like he was glad he'd risked his job to help me out.

Back out on the street, this time riding toward my destination for the meeting, I succumbed to the giddiness of near mishap, laughing at this big bike that had carried me back to fix my mistake. That's when his name came to me, that picture of me busting my lungs to get back to my backpack: Sprinter. It was a funny name considering his bulk, but it fit.

I rode south on Clark from the low retail buildings and wide open streets of the north side into the traffic-choked streets that wound below the towering skyscrapers of downtown. I'd been to Chicago a few times with my husband Jim to visit his sister and her husband, but never on a bike. From the bike I could taste the neighborhoods as I passed—Latino with shop after shop of colorful wears flowing onto the sidewalks, Scandinavian with soft hues and sweet aromas, the expectant pause around Wrigley Field as if the place itself was waiting for the next game. Over a bridge and into the canyons of downtown, Sprinter took to traffic well once I learned how to finesse his wide handlebar between cars.

The meeting over dinner at a glossy-bright Vietnamese restaurant south of downtown was a volley of the board chair's disconnected demands—some pertaining to the work plan format, some chiding me for questioning the 50/50 Project and the demands from the national organizations—until he seemed satisfied that I was going to fall back in line with his way of thinking. I got in a weak punch or two, saying he did not yet recognize me as the executive director of the organization, but for the most part he spoke and I nodded. We agreed to meet for breakfast to go over the final work plan format. I paid for my dinner and pedaled fast away.

I took the paved Lakefront Trail north, slowing my strokes as the distance grew, gliding through the twilight along the trail's curves between overhanging trees and through park lawns, leaning into Sprinter's bulk, then cut onto a street when the trail ended. I needed a beer, bad.

I found a brewpub on a street corner not far from where I was staying, the El train tracks looming a street width away. As a train clacked overhead, I locked Sprinter to a signpost with the coil lock I'd brought with me for the giveaway. The hoppy fragrance of the pint in my hand led me to the outside table I'd spotted when I rode up. The table sat in the corner of the patio, the inside edge of the sidewalk corner bordered by a low, wrought-iron fence. I set the pint down as I settled into the metal chair, ready for that first sip, but realized it wouldn't go down. Something was jammed in my throat. A weight pressed down on me. This trip, that ridiculous meeting, was all a farce. The board chair needed a puppet to jump to his commands and never question. The weight was my realization that I could never be his puppet, that Thunderhead could never be what I hoped it would be, that if I continued I would have to live a lie, that I had decided to continue, to do whatever it took to keep that job, my dream job, in hopes that I was wrong.

My gaze slipped from my beer looking glass to the street corner where an elderly black man had just gotten off a bus. A cigarette protruded from his lips as he raised his hand that must have held a lighter. His back was to me, a dusting of white in his hair. He froze, his hand halfway to the cigarette. For long seconds he stood like that as I half watched him, half struggled against the press and strangulation. He turned slowly, searching up the street, then his eyes fell on me. He froze again, then let his hand drop to his side as if the sight of me frightened him. Slowly, he removed the cigarette from his lips and carefully replaced it in the pack that rode in his breast pocket. More long seconds passed before he finally took deliberate steps toward me, concern creasing his face.

"What's wrong?" he asked when he reached the fence.

"Nothing," I lied, forcing the complex word through my constricted throat.

"Your sorrow hit me hard," he said. "Are you sure you're okay?"

"No," I said as the lump welled up and burst out as tears.

"I'm so sorry," he said. "Take care of yourself, okay?"

"Okay," I said as he turned and walked up the sidewalk and out of sight.

The next day, after the morning meeting, I agreed to give Sprinter to the board chair. I had told him about the Bike Hunt giveaway, that I planned to give Sprinter to someone who really needed him. He didn't care. He had devised a plan for his son to lock Sprinter at the end of his El train ride to school so he wouldn't have to walk the final blocks. I followed the board chair to his strange house off an alley northwest of downtown. It looked like a garage with rooms tacked onto it. Standing in their yard, I saw in the kid's eyes that he hated Sprinter and yet I relinquished him. This failed giveaway, the vision of Sprinter flung into their basement abandoned and despised by this boy, a waste of space in the family's eyes, was proof that I was losing myself. Without the giveaway, there is no Bike Hunt.

Back at work, it took me a full week to catch back up and deliver a work plan to the board that precisely followed the board chair's formatting. He didn't call. This finally allowed me to organize the November fundraiser in San Francisco. Gayle, the advocate from Texas who had knocked my socks off with her presentation at the Thunderhead Ranch, had offered her talents to the event planning. We booked a celebrity from the bike racing world, found a nice venue, and worked with the San Francisco bike organization to sell out the tickets. Aside from the venue changing our room the day of the event and the celebrity going missing until well into the show when he wandered in drunk, everyone had an excellent time and we raised significant money for Thunderhead.

I had found my bike at a thrift store in the Mission District on the way in from the airport. He was a blue twenty-inch-wheeled boy's bike with fat tires, six speeds, and a heavy-duty rear rack. I named him The Wedge when I used him to prop open a door while we were doing the final event prep. After the fundraiser, I stayed an extra day for bike rides and fun with the local bike advocates who had helped out.

On my last morning there, I allowed myself more than an hour for The Wedge's giveaway. I was staying with a local bike advocate in the Mission District and headed uphill from his place to Valencia Street. It was a Sunday morning, so I was worried that the people pickings might be a bit slim. As I rounded the corner onto Valencia, I spotted the father and two sons half a block away. The boys were maybe seven and eight, just above their father's waist. Initially, I ruled them out—two young boys, both would want The Wedge. But looking around at the nearly empty street, the shops sealed like sardine cans, the few vegetable stands void of customers, then back to the father as he joked with his boys, I reconsidered. Their clothes were faded and their shoes worn. Even one bike for both boys might be a windfall for them.

"Excuse me," I said, hoping they'd stop.

"Yes?" the father asked, as he came to a halt in front of me and his boys pulled up along side, studying me.

"I need to find a good home for this bike. I'm leaving today to return to Arizona where I live. I bought him at the thrift store on Mission. He's a great bike..."

As I rambled on, I realized the boys had shifted their attention to The Wedge. One reached out and carefully touched his handlebar. The other moved around back to push down on his rear rack.

"How much do you want for it?" the father asked in a disheartened tone, likely realizing his boys were already attached to the bike.

"Nothing, I just need to find someone who will promise to take care of him."

"Will you be back to get it?"

"No, no," I said, realizing my mistake, "the bike would be all yours...or your boys'...or one of your boy's." I had crossed into the uncharted territory. As the father's expression relaxed, I addressed the two boys, "Could you two share this bike?"

"Yeah!" they shouted in unison, jumping and dancing around the bike.

My concern was unwarranted. The father's delighted expression said it all. He thanked me and rolled the bike into one of his boys' hands. I handed the key for the lock to the other with as much ceremony. They turned and continued on their walk, one boy rolling The Wedge, the other skipping along side.

I thought of Sprinter as I watched The Wedge disappear down the sidewalk, a sting of guilt knowing that he too could have found a new owner who cherished him if only I had stayed true to the giveaway, and my heart.

That winter in Prescott, I endured more calls from the board chair, letting him talk, my palms sweating against the receiver, against his claims that I was naïve and had no idea what was actually going on. Of course, he had no intention of telling me. His cocky tone confirmed that he had shared these insults with the board, poisoning their belief in me.

Once the board had approved the work plan, he needed another topic. Over the past year I had protested suggestions from people outside of Thunderhead that we merge with other national organizations. They claimed there were too many national bike groups, not recognizing that Thunderhead was unique in its focus on serving local groups. Such a move would kill Thunderhead and its pride in separation from national efforts. During a board meeting where I had warned about one of these comments, the board chair latched on and began his push for a merger. The rest of the board became obsessed with the national organization he wanted to merge with as well as another, a bike industry association that they believed could fund the merger. Whole board meetings were spent discussing what these organizations were doing. The agenda items I had proposed for our programs were all but ignored. My protests only fueled him.

I moved ahead with our trainings anyway, finding willing host organizations, promoting them to our members, preparing trainers (all current or former leaders of local bicycle organizations), and creating materials that would cause attendees to work through the difficult stages of campaign planning. My goal was to conduct at least two of these multi-day trainings each year so that leaders of our member organizations would always have a chance to attend.

I scheduled the next at the end of March 2004 with the New York state organization in Albany. My early arrival in New York City gave me a chance to see the city and find a bike. I stayed with an advocate in Brooklyn and started my hunt from his apartment. Along a wide road lined with pawn and thrift shops I thought I'd find many bikes to choose from. But the grumpy guy in the fourth shop said my best bet would be a quirky bike shop that had no sign out front. I'd have to knock on the door if it was locked.

I found Victoria under a massive heap of broken bikes behind that shop after an elderly man let me in. She was a sleek metallic-blue girl's-frame Schwinn with tall, skinny wheels and a pedal-back brake. She'd caught my eye as soon as I stepped into the muddy yard. It took me lots of yanking and repiling of other bikes to pull her free. She was ready to go. I wondered, as I paid the shop owner the twenty dollars, if he'd later regret letting such a beauty go so cheap.

The training in Albany became our next step for our campaign training model. I'd worked with the trainers from the year before to improve the course outline and focus more on campaigns. I hired each of these trainers as job-specific contractors as most still held jobs at their bicycle advocacy organizations. By shifting from organization development and fundraising to campaigns for improving their communities for bicycling, we actually did a better job with organization development and fundraising. With the focus on impact, attendees had to solve their organization and funding concerns. Without a strong membership, brand, or promotion plan, an organization had no chance of causing significant change. And without the funding to counter an opposition attack, a campaign would be dead in the water before it began. As the Albany training wrapped up with all attendees charged and ready to implement bold campaigns, we knew we'd hit on the right formula.

Back in New York City, Victoria's giveaway was surprisingly difficult—another Sunday morning like The Wedge's giveaway the November before. The streets of Brooklyn were nearly vacant, though it was a bright spring day. I was joined by the local bicycle advocate I'd stayed with. He wanted to see what this Bike Hunt giveaway was about. After wandering for many blocks, I remembered the little neighborhood parks I'd passed during my stay, always buzzing with kids and parents. We headed to the closest park. Rounding the corner my hope returned. Inside the tall metal fence, benches were interspersed with people keeping watch on their kids. I entered at the gate and turned to two women sitting together on the first bench, khakis and jeans, one with a head scarf, the other with her frizzy black hair tied for a controlled burst at the back. After listening to my spiel, the woman with her hair tied back placed her hand on her heart.

"You mean you would give this beautiful bike to me?"

"Yes," I said, barely controlling my own excitement. "In fact, I would be thrilled to give her to you."

Still sitting, she reached for Victoria's handlebar gazing at her. I let Victoria go and stood back, no longer in her vision. Her friend told me her bike had been stolen many months before and she didn't have the money to buy a new one. This reminded me.

"She comes with a lock," I said, as I fished for the key and then handed it to her.

"I'm stunned," she said. "For me?"

"Yes," I said, "she's all yours. I named her Victoria because she's so beautiful."

"That's a perfect name for her," she said. "I'll take very good care of her."

I bid them farewell, including the advocate who lingered there, glided out of the gate and back to my travel schedule, back to Prescott, back to helping the local leaders.

Our next and last training for 2004 was held in April in Chicago at the office of the board chair's local bicycle organization. I enjoyed the training, even with the board chair dominating the room. The Midwest region was terribly void of effective bicycle organizations at that time, so I'd put a lot of effort into inviting people interested in leading new organizations. In attendance were curious new advocates from Missouri, Iowa, Minnesota, Kentucky, Kansas, Michigan, and even as far away as Idaho. The rest of the forty registrants came from existing, successful organizations so my new ducklings had lots of mentors to connect with.

The board chair let me ride Sprinter while I was there. I'd found Sprinter covered in dust in the basement of his house, just as I had expected, and had to return him to that same spot when I left.

For my next trip, I'd found an excuse to return to Europe. Nine years had passed since I was last there. I had discovered the European Cyclists' Federation (ECF) during my campaign research, a coalition like Thunderhead of bicycle organizations throughout Europe. We could surely learn a lot from each other. In order for Thunderhead to join ECF, I had to attend ECF's annual general meeting in Madrid that June and present our case to their members for a vote. Then, of course, I could take a short flight to Sweden to be with my adopted family.

Even though I would pay for the entire trip with my own money, the board denied my request. Ten days away was unacceptable. Finally, after many phone calls and emails they approved the trip.

The Bike Hunt in Madrid was the most difficult yet. I started the morning of my arrival after checking in at the hostel where the ECF meeting attendees were staying. Jet lag slowed my every move. The muggy June heat steeped my headache. For hours I asked everyone I came to, first in English and then with a few words from my Spanish dictionary. Through the cobbled, narrow streets of downtown lined with playfully adorned buildings, then out into the neighborhoods with wide streets and speeding traffic, I discovered the diversity of Madrid. I could barely speak English through my exhaustion and nobody I encountered could at all. By five o'clock I was nearly crawling up a sloped sidewalk on my way back to the hostel, trying to comprehend a failed hunt, when a man on a bicycle shot from a side street onto the sidewalk and directly at me.

"Stop!" I said, the most international word I could think of.

He stopped and I held him in place with all the jumbled Spanish words I had gathered along my convoluted route that day, hoping he would point me toward a place that could sell me a bike. To my surprise, he stepped off his bike and pushed it toward me like he would be glad to be rid of it. He pointed to the rear derailleur that stuck nearly straight out. I wondered if I'd have to make the bike a one speed. He wiggled the loose wheels and gestured at the bike as if it had attacked him. He clearly hated it. He held up three fingers then made a zero for how many euros he wanted, but I had no problem talking him down to twenty—about thirty dollars at the time. He took the money and walked away down the hill in the direction he had been heading. And there I stood with Sidewalk Sam. Finally I had a bike. I could hardly believe it.

My last stop along the hunt before this encounter had been a bike shop near the bottom of the hill. The owner had wanted to help though he had no used bikes, so I jumped on Sam to coast down carefully, hoping the shop was still open. The owner was glad to let me use his tools to work on the bike out on the sidewalk. I fixed the derailleur by laying Sam down on his side and standing on the derailleur body until it was once again parallel to the bike. Amazingly, this worked. All his other ailments were easy to fix.

The next four days were filled with meetings and bike rides with the leaders of bicycle advocacy organizations from nearly twenty European countries. On the first day of the meeting, representatives of candidate organizations had to give our presentations. I fought my nerves as we all gathered in the courtyard surrounded by the hostel's dormitory buildings, the lush green trees blocking the early morning sun, denying the June heat. The meeting was to take place in a police station a short walk from the hostel—not the meeting room planned by the host organization, but a workable last-minute solution. The police had offered their windowless, low-ceilinged, fluorescent-lit training room with several half circles of strange high-backed bright blue chairs that resembled airplane seats. The half circles faced a sort of stage where a long wooden desk displayed the police station shield. Behind and to the side of that desk sat the members of the ECF Management Committee, their board of directors, who presided over the multi-day meeting.

I had to stand in front of the stage in the midst of the members perched in those weird blue chairs to deliver my overview of Thunderhead and why I believed connecting the two organizations would be mutually beneficial. After a few more presentations, all votes were in favor. Thunderhead was an official member of the European Cyclists' Federation (ECF).

During the rest of the meeting as well as along the bike rides that followed, I learned new ideas about how my European colleagues were increasing bicycle ridership in their home countries. I also thrilled at the odd sensation of respect. I hadn't realized how demoralizing the Thunderhead board's attitude toward me had become. Every time they demanded I prove what I presented—results from trainings, interest from potential new partners, requests from members—something had eroded in me. There in Madrid, the ECF board and members treating me like their colleague revealed a disturbing, but ever so appreciated contrast. They were as intrigued to learn from me as I was to learn from them.

On one ride that wound along a path next to a small river, I rode next to an advocate from the Netherlands, asking her about their national policy that assumes the driver of a motorized vehicle is always guilty in a crash with a bicyclist or pedestrian. Genius. To have such a backdrop at the national level in the United States would change everything from street designs to people's attitudes about bicycling. Even if just a city or state could pass such a policy, it would shift all bicycle campaigns forward for that area.

Many other policies and initiatives I learned about also set bicyclists out as superior to drivers of motor vehicles. Bicycle roads in Germany were specifically designed to make driving inconvenient and bicycling most convenient. Neighborhood zones in Switzerland set speed limits below twenty miles per hour and pinched streets so that cars could not drive fast even if they wanted to. I took pages of notes and gathered a pile of brochures from these organizations to bring back to Thunderhead members.

That trip was also my first encounter with the problems surrounding bicycle helmets. I'd never worn a helmet as a bike messenger, had never even considered them until I got my apprentice job at a bike shop in Prescott before I opened my own shop. The owner taught me to push every customer to buy a helmet with terrifying questions like, "How much is your head worth?" or "Won't you regret not buying this helmet when your child crashes?" We implanted the idea that riding a bicycle was sure to end in a horrific crash and, without a helmet, that crash would lead to death or brain damage. For some reason, I never questioned this and carried those offensive lines over to my shop.

A handful of these Europeans had begun a campaign to counter overzealous bicycle helmet promotions that were setting bicycling out as far more dangerous than it actually is, thus deterring people from bicycling. On a ride up to a hilltop park shaded by tall, bulbous, twisted and sculpted pine trees overlooking the spreading metropolis of Madrid, I found myself in the midst of a group discussing their next steps for this campaign. The helmet on my head pressed my temples and increased in weight as I listened. Mine was the only helmet along on that ride of about forty. I wanted to fling it over the wall into the city below, but instead let it sit on top of me like a cumbersome display of the problem.

I learned as I pedaled and listened how little protection bicycle helmets offer. They are only designed to protect the top of the head and to a total impact velocity of thirteen miles per hour, the speed a head reaches if the person falls over from a standstill. Also, a helmet cannot prevent brain damage caused by the shifting of the brain inside the skull. Yet helmet promoters and manufacturers present bicycle helmets as a means to prevent all head injuries, even in a crash with a motor vehicle. A complete scam. I hate being scammed.

On the last day with them, as we once again gathered in the hostel's courtyard to say our goodbyes and pedal our separate ways, I asked an advocate who had been part of that discussion if I could join their Helmet Working Group to help counter this menace to the bicycle advocacy movement. He and the others welcomed me and noted with a few friendly jeers that I'd packed my helmet away.

My Swedish brother Knut picked me up at the airport near Stockholm and we didn't stop talking for the entire hour-long drive, trying to catch up. I kept looking over, soaking in the sight of him, potato dust softening the new grey in his ruffled brown hair and beard that ringed his tough, but kind face, the same thick-rimmed glasses perched on his strong nose, his beefy, grease-stained hands gesturing from the steering wheel as he told the latest stories from the farm. When we drove up to the main farm house, my Swedish parents, Per and Marianne, rushed out and waited for me to open the car door so they could fight for the first hug.

I remember those five days back on the farm like an early Technicolor movie, the colors clearer and brighter than possible. The red of the houses and farm buildings, the green of the grass and trees, the silver of the gravel road that wends between the two farms they own, and of course all the faces of these dear people—other family members, kids, neighbors, farmers from nearby, villagers, and workers I'd worked with and known all those years before. I savored every sight, sound, voice, smell, and taste. These were the people who had showed me what the word family meant, what the hype was all about. Most people know it from the beginning, but I discovered them, my true family, in my late teens, so they are all the more precious to me.

Marianne made my favorite meals including her famous meatballs (half pork, half moose) and her secret lasagna recipe using an Ethiopian spice. The first night, actually the next morning, when I finally forced myself to go to bed, I lay on the bed I'd slept in all those harvest seasons as a farm worker, upstairs in Marianne and Per's house, listening, smelling, staring wide-eyed out the window in the soft summer light that never allowed total darkness, watching that same tree, its tiny heart-shaped leaves flittering in the night wind. I lifted my hand to the wall to caress the textured wallpaper that was like vertical strips of yellow-brown yarn. So many nights I had crawled into that bed exhausted after a hard day of work and touched that wall before dropping into a deep sleep. Sleep didn't come so easily during my visit because I didn't want to miss a minute of being there.

During meals and coffee breaks when Knut and the others asked me to explain my new job, I did my best to tell them. They had understood why I couldn't visit as my bike shop was growing. A few of them had come to Prescott during those nine years when I couldn't visit them. But explaining my Thunderhead job proved a lot more difficult. I told them about all the emails and phone calls, the board meetings where I had to prove everything over and over again, the trainings, the national meetings in Washington, D.C. Knut asked why I had to do all this constant work, what I was accomplishing. I realized he was trying to relate it to his work—prepare the fields, plant, harvest. To him, I had spent the last two years only preparing the fields. His crinkled brow reminded me of the time at the Thunderhead Ranch I'd tried to tell that river guide joke to the board members. They didn't understand me or my past. Now, the people from my past who did care about me, didn't understand my present.

When the last day arrived all too soon, I had to force myself to pack and say goodbye. With all the work that was waiting for me, I was anxious to get back to Prescott, but my heart longed to stay at Hillsta where I was valued. I left Sam with them to become a farm bike transporting Knut and his workers between the farms.

The rest of the summer I played catch-up in my home office, following up from our spring trainings and offering what I'd learned in Europe to Thunderhead members. I also had to prepare for our next retreat coming up in September in Victoria, British Columbia, prior to a bicycle conference that was also being held in Victoria.

At the same time, I was still serving on the board of PAT, without much time to offer. I mostly reviewed documents and suggested ideas, but could not participate in any events. I also still owned the bike shop. One evening after my husband Jim came home from the motorcycle shop he owns and operates, he began telling me ways to improve the merchandising at my bike shop.

"You want to buy it?" I asked.

"Your bike shop?" he asked.

"Yeah, do you want to buy my bike shop?"

"Yes."

"Five dollars."

He pulled out a five dollar bill. I took it and the shop was his. After thirteen years owning and operating that bike shop, I was released from it and all its accompanying responsibilities. This lightening of my load did not last long as the demands of my Thunderhead job soon filled it.

A few days before the retreat in Victoria was to begin, I flew into Seattle where I planned on hunting for a bike before taking a ferry to Victoria. I stayed with a local bike advocate who was also on the Thunderhead board. That evening in her living room, we discussed involving members in committees, creating new member resources, and enlisting the retreat attendees in all our programs. Being there with her complicated my misgivings about the board members. Her warm welcome and our fun chats as we caught up reassured me that maybe she and the others were not actually buying into the merger idea.

The next morning, I started on the Bike Hunt in downtown Seattle after walking there from her house. Following my first helper's directions to a pawn shop near the fish market, I found they had no bikes and had no idea where I could get one. There were so many bikes zipping by me, I was confident I'd find a bike in no time. I had the whole day because we didn't have to leave for Victoria until the next. Having a full day away from the constant pressure of my job was a welcome break. So I sauntered through the length of the fish market, taking in the displays and the views of the water, before asking again.

I'd forgotten the Bike Hunt rule that the hunt always takes all the time you have. By late afternoon, I had inquired at more than a dozen pawn shops, three bike shops, and a thrift store. I was at what appeared to be the southern end of the city—a wasteland of industrial tanks, blank buildings, and dusty lots, crisscrossed by monstrous freeway flyovers, not a soul in sight. I turned back around with a sinking heart, knowing that I had swept the entire narrow city. My legs became lead as I realized I'd been walking that whole day, trudging up the east slope then back down toward the water, and had no bike to show for it. Backtracking along the dead street, I remembered a bustling coffee shop before the street had fallen silent. It was nestled next to a wedge of park at the intersection of three angled streets, outside tables crowded with people, bikes propped and lying amongst them. Someone there had to know where I could find a bike.

The eight teenagers crowded around the table I approached all agreed that the Goodwill two blocks away was my best bet. I argued, defying the Bike Hunt rule that once they point you in a direction, no matter how crazy it sounds, you must follow their lead to the end. I was sure I'd been to that thrift store and described it to prove them wrong. Eight heads shook insistently. That was another one a few blocks in another direction. Finally I succumbed, thanked them and headed in the direction of their pointing fingers.

Forcing my leaden legs forward, I wound my way through the clothes racks and stench of stale perfume toward the back of the Goodwill where I figured bikes might be. At the end of the last aisle, my eyes fell on a wondrous sight—a mound of bikes, twisted and tangled. I pried myself from the spot, needing desperately to believe the oasis. At the top of the stack were garbage mass-merchant bikes—Huffys, Murrays, Roadmasters, the sorts I like to call BSOs (bicycle shaped objects) with pressed-together frames and brittle plastic brake levers. I pulled them off the pile and set them aside, hoping I wouldn't have to settle for one of them.

And there she was, mid-stack, her fire-engine-red frame a beacon amidst the debris, a classic men's-frame Nishiki mountain bike from the mid '80s with all her original, quality Suntour parts—indexed shifters, derailleurs, brakes, and high-flanged, gorgeous hubs. I froze, taking her in as I kept my ears alert for anyone approaching. Thankfully no one risked the bodily harm I would have inflicted had they dared to approach her. I paid the same ten dollars that was stuck to all the bikes and rushed out the door before anyone could realize the treasure they'd just let go.

I named her Jane almost immediately. Maybe it was her bright red color or her meticulousness, hardly a scratch and every part perfect, oiled, loved. The owner who had coddled her must have died because otherwise they never would have let her end up under that stack of BSOs at that Goodwill.

I arrived at the retreat center outside of Victoria with most of the board members. The woodsy complex of low, roughhewn buildings sat in a forest clearing with a vast, trimmed lawn behind. Before the retreat started, we held a short board meeting in the naturally lit main room of the lodge. The meeting soon spun away from the agenda as usual to harp on the merger, all speculation and gossip. Clearly, none of the leaders of the other two organizations had been approached. During the few focused moments, we tackled some hard issues like adding pedestrian advocacy to Thunderhead's mission.

The retreat clicked through its planned paces without a problem, but lacked the life and camaraderie I had missed since the 2002 retreat, though our members once again gave stellar presentations. There were about the same number of registrants as attended the year before, just over fifty, but fortunately only a few were representatives of the national organizations. In between the retreat sessions, the board chair organized competitive Frisbee games, pitting one team against the other. Attendees seemed to enjoy playing and watching so I didn't try to organize any other activities. Any enthusiasm I may have brought with me for engaging our members had been stomped out on the morning of the first full day.

I am outside the forest lodge. The edge of the expansive lawn that spreads away to a wall of spruce trees is lined with the leaders of our member organizations sitting in the grass facing me, eager to start the annual meeting. Thunderhead members are organizations, not just people, so I know these leaders represent far more than themselves. Their impression of the retreat equals their impression of Thunderhead and will follow them back to their constituents. As I begin my carefully prepared introduction of why we are there, ready to lead into the day's activities, the board chair steps in front of me, edits my previous statement and changes the subject. I let him finish, thank him and start again a few steps away. He steps in front of me again and starts on a new topic. The third time he steps in front of me, I walk away.

I kept to the edges for the rest of the retreat and avoided him during the bicycle conference.

On my last morning after the conference in Victoria that followed the retreat, I walked out onto the sidewalk in front of the conference venue with Jane at my side. Jane deserved to find a home like her original owner must have given her, someone who would care for her and appreciate how special she was. I started down the wide, landscaped sidewalk, past caringly pruned young trees and flower boxes, benches and public art. I'd never seen such an adorned city, designed first for flowers and trees, a fitting place for Jane.

The people I passed all seemed content and busy with their tasks. I'd only walked a few blocks when I spotted him, a somewhat overweight middle-aged man dressed in colorful rags, settled on a bench, his dreadlocks bundled under a billowing knitted cap of yellow, red, and green. I stopped to figure out what he was doing. He was counting change in his palm. With careful steps I approached, trying not to startle him in his vulnerable task. I stopped again about ten feet away and waited, watching his dark finger as it moved each coin to the edge of his palm. The finger froze on a silver coin and he looked up, his brilliant green eyes electrifying me.

"Sorry," I said, "I didn't mean to interrupt you."

"It's okay," he said. "I'm afraid I don't have enough anyway. How can I help you?"

"I need to find someone who needs a bike, who can take care of this bike, who..." my emotion got the better of me.

"Can you start again? I'm not quite sure what you're getting at," he said in a soothing voice.

"Would you like this bike?" I blurted.

"I would love that bike," he said with conviction.

"She's all yours," I said, then realized this man had no idea of the background. I was so concerned about finding Jane a great home, I had completely blown my giveaway spiel. I quickly filled in the missing parts about finding her at the Goodwill in Seattle and riding her during my week of meetings, that I had to find her a new home because I was leaving for my home in Arizona in a few hours. As I spoke, his face gradually shifted from his serious change-counting expression to jubilation. I rolled Jane close enough so he could reach her handlebar then let her go when he reached out. "She's a beauty," I said, "All original, a classic mountain bike from the mid '80s."

"I can see she's a beauty," he said as he studied her.

"I'm so glad you can give her a good home. And here's the key to her lock."

"It's my pleasure to give her a home," he said, carefully taking the key. "In fact, you have given me exactly what I needed most. When you approached, I was counting my money to see if I had enough for one bus ride. Now, with this bike, I will never have to pay for a bus trip again."

I could only smile in response because I couldn't find any words.

"Now, there's just one more thing I want," he said, fixing his eyes on mine. "I want you to get exactly what you need too. I will pray for this, that you get exactly what you need."

As I stood there, captivated by his green, determined eyes, I wondered what that might be. All my reference points had been replaced with what I believed Thunderhead needed. I let his words be the last between us, nodded with appreciation, and left him and Jane together on that majestic street.

Two months later on November 1st, 2004, I stepped out of a youth hostel in downtown Chicago with Sprinter by my side. It was the end of a quick, nearly disastrous trip that had centered around another fundraiser for Thunderhead. Like the San Francisco fundraiser, I had expected the Chicago bike advocates to step forward in droves to lend a hand, encouraged to help by the board chair. He was also a leader of the local Chicago bicycle advocacy organization, so he had the means to mobilize a small army and he had assured me he would. This is why I had organized the fundraiser in Chicago. Instead, a month before the event, after I'd reserved the room, secured auction items, and scheduled the speakers, not one of the local bike advocates had helped with ticket sales, promotions, or spreading the word. In the end it was all I could do to get a few dozen people to attend the expensive affair, even resorting to begging my in-laws to help fill the room.

At the event, after the presentation of a big check from an industry sponsor who would have given it anyway and having introduced the next speaker, I nervously worked the sparse room wishing I had rented a smaller one so it would look more crowded, greeting each precious attendee like royalty. Thunderhead ended up losing money, but thankfully not much.

When I'd arrived in Chicago, I'd simply gone to the board chair's house and taken Sprinter. I'd told him I was going to do this via email, in statement form, not a question. His wife seemed relieved to get rid of the hefty bike. I was relieved to have him back under my care.

That last morning, I stepped out into the chilly November air, a light drizzle falling. It was just past seven o'clock, a Monday morning. Even though it was a weekday, I knew my prospects would be slim in such miserable weather. I swung my leg over, took a few pedal strokes, and let Sprinter roll off the curb into the nearly empty street. I headed south because that's where I'd seen the most people who seemed to be struggling, some homeless with bedrolls, others worn out from life's relentless attacks.

I saw him after several long blocks, his back to me, facing a fence to get a pocket of dry air to light his cigarette. He wasn't quite frail, not quite old, but definitely sad. I veered across the four lanes of the wide street and bounced up onto the sidewalk, easing Sprinter to a stop not far from him. I gave my spiel as soon as he turned, unlit cigarette back in his hand as he took in my words.

"Heck yeah, I need a bike!"

I'd found Sprinter's new home. It took me over a year, but I did it. Maybe this is what I needed, what that green-eyed man in Victoria had prayed for me to get.

"Okay," I said, as I rolled Sprinter close enough so he could grab the handlebar, "he's your bike now."

But he didn't reach out. Instead he recoiled and stepped back to cower next to the fence, his eyes terrified, looking past me. I turned to find a muscular youth towering over me.

"You gonna give *him* that bike?" the punk spat.

"I already did," I said.

"Give it to me," the punk said.

"It's okay, it's okay," the man stammered. "I really don't need a bike. He can have it." He turned and began walking away.

"Wait," I said, maybe a bit too loud, "come back here. This

is your bike. I don't know who the fuck this guy is, but he sure as hell isn't getting this bike!" This was Sprinter, damn it, and I wasn't going to let any more bullies take him from me.

I turned to glare at the punk. Fire must have been shooting out of my eyes because he stepped back. I turned to find the timid man shuffling back toward me through the misty rain.

"You sure it's mine?" he said, half asking, half convincing himself.

"Damn straight this bike is yours! And don't ever let anyone take him away from you. Promise me that."

"I promise," he said, his grin returning as he finally took hold of the handlebar, swung his leg over, grabbed the key from my outstretched hand, and rode away, back straight and proud. When I turned around, the bully had vanished.

6
Power Gauge

I began to notice patterns of trauma that the local organizations were suffering—ruptures in leadership teams, witch hunts. On such calls, I learned to listen and not judge, asking questions until I could understand the beginning and how they had reached that point. I usually discovered with dismay that their bylaws supported this behavior and recognized the language, copied and pasted from national nonprofit associations. These bylaws set the executive director out as inferior to the board, not a team member, only a tool to hire and fire. I checked nonprofit laws and consulted with nonprofit attorneys, but found no requirement for such language.

Each call helped me decipher the next—a rogue leader, confused roles, rumors and lies. I could then guide them back to working as a team. I also pushed them to rewrite their bylaws, but most dropped the idea once their situation improved.

Word got out and the calls from our members increased, most ending well. While happy endings boosted my ego, the patterns disturbed me. Why were so many leadership teams tearing each other apart? While I'd seen some of this sort of infighting and dysfunction in the other nonprofits I'd worked for, I'd expected better in the bicycle movement.

At conferences and events outside of the bicycle advocacy movement, I only had to begin my description of these patterns and whoever I was speaking to would break in with a similar, personal story. The realization that most nonprofits were suffering from infighting did not lessen my concern. Other movements were far more established and could weather disruptions.

As my fascination and disturbance with group behavior grew, I found even more solace in my Bike Hunts. In January of 2005, three months after that exhilarating giveaway of Sprinter, I was in Miami, my first visit to that city. I had secured a booth space for Thunderhead at a conference on environmentally friendly development methods referred to as smart-growth. Gayle joined me. We set up the booth the morning before the conference began. Standing back, we both agreed it needed something to catch the eye. My hunt for a bike would soon solve this problem.

The hunt led me first to a bike shop, then onto a bus to North Miami where the best pawn shops were supposed to be. From my sideways seat near the front of the bus, I could spot the ocean off to the right. If I looked across the aisle and way back to the left, I could see the cluster of spires that was downtown Miami. We crossed a bridge over an inlet where sailboats mixed with commercial fishing boats. I looked for the familiar crab pots and hoists I knew from my crabbing days in San Francisco, but only saw seine nets. As we entered the cluttered neighborhoods of North Miami, the low buildings a mix of bargain stores and auto-body shops, I perched on the edge of my seat searching through all the bus windows for a pawn shop. I let the bus roll past one, then another, chiding myself for not getting out, then looking ahead, hoping to see a line of bikes on the sidewalk.

"What are you looking for?"

The voice bewildered me until I focused back inside the bus where a round woman in a soft orange dress was leaning across the aisle to speak to me.

"Oh, hi," I said, stalling to regain my grasp of my immediate surroundings. "Yeah, I am looking for something. Do you by chance know where I could find a used bike around here? Someone said there were good pawn shops in this neighborhood that might sell bikes."

"Sure!" she said, obviously thrilled that my problem was one she could help solve. "But don't bother with these darn pawn shops. Am I right?" This question was directed at the other passengers who returned sounds and nods of agreement. "You follow me," she said leaning back across the aisle to me, "and I'll show you where you can get a bike." She winked at the other passengers who nodded back.

After a few more blocks, we got off the bus together. Though she walked with a cane, I had to work to keep up. She darted between two buildings, one a pawn shop, then crossed a wide parking lot before turning left into a shadowed alley, never looking back to make sure I was with her. Well ahead of me, she stopped in an asphalt clearing and turned back with a triumphant sweep of her arm.

"There you go," she said. "You're sure to find a bike in there."

I followed her gesture to an enormous Goodwill storefront, hidden from the main street. I never would have found it on my own. I thanked her for taking such good care of me and then headed toward the door. When I looked back, she was gone.

At the rear of the store my eyes landed on the brightest, pinkest bike I had ever seen. She was a twenty-inch-wheeled girl's BMX-style bike with white tires and crank arms to highlight her hot pink frame and fork. Even her rims were hot pink. After paying the five dollars, I wheeled her across the side street to a muffler shop where the mechanic let me air up her tires. He didn't have any tools to lend, but pointed me to the body shop next door. The group of four body shop workers were so entertained by my mechanic skills with my bright pink bike that they lent me any tool I needed. I adjusted her hubs and headset, raised and tightened her handlebar and seat, tightened her chain and axle nuts, then took her for a quick spin around their work area to test the pedal-back brake. They clapped as I waved my thanks and shot out onto the street. The name Peaches came to me as I pedaled her back south along the busy main road, a fitting name for a bike who loved the limelight. She completed our conference booth, perched at its edge, a conversation starter for anyone with a bike story.

On the last evening there, after Gayle and I packed up the

booth and dealt with the shipping service, I wheeled Peaches out the front door to find her new home. It was already dark and I worried that anyone I approached might be even more suspicious of me than usual when trying to give away a bike. I pedaled Peaches carefully along the busy, multi-lane road, the typical road type I'd seen all over the area. No wonder there were so few people riding bicycles there. Cars swept past my left shoulder as I focused on keeping the handlebar straight, scanning the sidewalks for someone who would adore Peaches. The few people out were rushing somewhere else, no time for a bright pink bike. I rode on into the night, heading west away from the city and into hardened neighborhoods where iron bars were favored over business signs.

Ahead, three small figures were walking much slower than the other people I'd seen. They were speaking softly as they walked, looking at each other rather than the sidewalk. One was likely the mother, barely five feet tall. The boy was only a bit smaller than she was, perhaps ten years old. The smallest was a young girl and she had on a pink coat. I swear Peaches sped up as soon as I spotted them, but I pedaled back to slow down. I didn't want to startle them so I eased onto the sidewalk at the next driveway and got off to walk toward them.

"Excuse me," I said, and watched with dismay as they all jumped back in fright. "I'm sorry, I didn't mean to scare you."

The boy whispered in Spanish to his sister and mother and they both nodded at him. "It's okay," he said, and stepped in front to lead them past me.

"Just a minute," I said, "can I ask you something?"

"Yes, of course," he said as he stopped to listen.

I gave him my giveaway spiel and suggested maybe his sister would like the bike. When I had finished, he nodded to show he understood, then turned to the other two to translate, taking his role as translator and negotiator very seriously. As he retold my story in Spanish, both of their faces brightened, and when he came to the end, the girl jumped up and down, still staring up into her brother's face as if to make sure he'd really said it. The mother began speaking very rapidly as the boy encouraged her with "si, si."

He turned back to me. "My sister would be very happy to accept the bicycle," he said in a business-like tone, "and my mother would like to thank you very much. You see, yesterday was my sister's eighth birthday and she had hoped for a bicycle."

The Bike Hunt had succeeded yet again.

During that spring of 2005, I began sorting out the patterns of conflicts I was increasingly responding to, then came up with names for some of the most common.

"Renter's Syndrome" was my term for new board and staff members tearing down existing organization structures—new name, new mission, new programs. I rented out the house next to my original bike shop. Often within the first month of moving in my tenants would discard good appliances, tear out walls and even wiring. People tend to change things that are new to them. Only explicit rules and my assurance that I would evict them if they made any changes to the property prevented this behavior. My recommendations to organization leaders were the same—strengthen your policies to protect the structure and good work of the organization.

"The Dangerous Doldrums" described the apathy of leaders who discovered that the sky didn't fall if they chose not to do anything. They'd meet and discuss bicycle campaigns and programs, realized they'd take a lot of work, and do nothing. Nothing bad happened, just as nothing bad happened to the captain and sailors on the ships stuck in the windless doldrums of the ocean. They languished there until they died. I learned the hard way that the same fate awaits organizations. Their phones are disconnected and their websites vanish. This syndrome is so comfortable that even my suggested remedies proved too much trouble.

The "Anchor Control Syndrome" described the aftereffect of a power grab when a leader had won control of an organization and then prevented it from accomplishing anything. The result appears the same as the Dangerous Doldrums—the organization comes to a standstill. But the internal struggle is far different. With the Anchor Control Syndrome, one dynamic individual has dropped anchor and is daring the others to challenge him or her. Usually they don't. Instead, they walk away, the board dwindles to a few who never cared anyway, and the organization grinds to a halt. Surprisingly, I had more luck guiding leaders out of this syndrome than the Dangerous Doldrums *because* of this internal conflict. As long as at least one of the leaders cared about the organization, there was a chance they would call for my assistance.

These studies were not part of the approved work plan. The board was pushing for studies on bike riding, not the enigmas of human behavior. They wanted all my program time focused on filling 50/50 Project gaps, surveying our members for the national organizations, winning bicycle industry funding, and compiling bike-riding statistics.

During that spring of 2005, my frustration was tempered by two Bike Hunts. In March, two months after Peaches, I found myself back in Chicago to participate in a workshop hosted by the local bicycle advocacy organization for its members. This time I was set on completing a Bike Hunt in Chicago.

The hunt took three hours, starting with a long, enlightening walk far south of the city—prison-like housing projects, some groups helpful, others toying with me, a feeling like I was the most interesting sight all day. I followed the zigzag directions of my helpers to a bike shop north of the city where I found Penelope, an all-original, royal blue mid-1950s Sears single-speed with a pedal-back brake, perfect for slicing through Chicago's traffic.

The morning after the workshop, which was not as interesting as I had hoped, I headed south to give away Penelope, just as I'd done with Sprinter—a Sunday morning with only one hour to find her a home. The streets were deserted save for a few cars. I turned onto side streets hoping to find a park or other place where people gathered. Nothing. Back onto the thoroughfare heading south, all I could see into the morning glare was miles of vacant sidewalk. My pedal strokes slowed. The farther I pedaled, the farther I'd have to walk, or pedal, back. A thick shadow from a hulking freeway flyover crossed the wasteland of blinding pavement. I was drawn to the shadow more for relief than hope.

They appeared as my eyesight adjusted, a line of about thirty forlorn people behind a van with its double rear doors wide open, stuffed with loaves of bread. From drought to flood. How was I going to approach thirty people, all of whom likely needed Penelope? I didn't have time to worry about it. I followed my instincts as usual, pedaling slowly up to the line then coasting along its length, waiting for a sign.

"Good morning," said a young, battered man with blond hair and beard. "Nice bike you have there."

And we've found our winner. I slammed on the brakes. "Do you need a bike?" I asked him.

"I sure do!"

"Well," I said as I stepped off and leaned Penelope toward him, "it would be my pleasure to give you this bike."

He listened, stunned, as I gave him the spiel. As I handed him the key, the people on both sides of him in the line patted his shoulders and congratulated him, some calling him James. He thanked me with his eyes before I turned away, still enjoying their celebratory chatter as I rounded the corner to begin my long walk back to the hostel. I was on a different street from the one I had come south on, peeking into storefronts and windows I wouldn't have noticed earlier through my frustration.

Crossing a side street, I saw a homeless shelter a few blocks down with a small group of people gathered outside talking and soaking up the sun. Good to know I would have had an option if I hadn't found that breadline. Just as I stepped up onto the curb, just before the shelter would have vanished from my view, I caught a glimpse of movement, a flash of blue and that unmistakable blond beard. I stopped, one foot in the street, the other on the curb to watch a beaming James ride up to his buddies. He'd left the breadline to show off his new wheels. That guy had his priorities straight.

Back in Prescott on the monthly board meeting conference call, my bags not yet unpacked, the board chair requested a review of my performance complete with a review committee, audits of financials and program results, multiple meetings, and publishing the results. Such a process, just as our trainings were starting, would have compromised those events and set everything back by months. The other board members responded that they were pleased with my performance and that reviews should be done at yearend. They may not have been pitching in to help much, but I was glad they had my back on this one.

One month later, in April 2005, I was in Portland, Oregon to conduct our next training. Neither the hunt nor the giveaway turned out as I expected. For the hunt, I had figured that finding a bike in one of the most bike-friendly United States cities would be a cinch. Not so. In downtown, everyone had a bike and none of the shops could keep a used bike in stock. Also, something disturbed me there. Everything was a bit too clean, a bit too perfect. My suspicion of the place hit home when I asked a black woman working behind the counter of a Goodwill where she thought I could find a used bike nearby.

"Honey," she laughed, "do you really think that *I* would know anything about this area? I can't afford to *live* here."

That's when I realized she was the first non-white, non-fashionably-dressed person I had encountered in hours of traversing the city. I asked her where a better part of town would be. Not a better part of town to find a bike, just a better part of town. She knew what I meant. I followed her directions north and got off the bus when I finally started seeing weeds, cracks in sidewalks, and a variety of people. After walking several blocks I found a house with a yard full of bikes. The owner was an eccentric tinkerer named Dingo who especially loved making art out of bikes and was glad to sell me one. The chrome BMX I chose was one of the few still intact. Of course I named him Dingo.

The training went well, though it hadn't attracted as many participants as other trainings. I wondered if this was because bicycle advocates in that area took bicycling for granted. Still, we brought in advocates from as far away as Mississippi and those in attendance appreciated the material. By then, leaders from most of our nearly 120 member organizations had participated in at least one training or retreat and many had attended multiple times, bringing along their peers to share the experience.

Giving away a bike in a city where everyone already has one should be a real challenge, right? Again I was wrong. Not far from where I was staying downtown, as I rode Dingo slowly, carefully looking for the slightest opportunity, a young boy ran across my path.

"Hey," I shouted.

He stopped and turned around. "What."

"You want a bike?"

"Yeah," he said as he walked up to me.

"Okay, he's all yours. I bought him from an artist north of the city and now I have to leave town to head back to my home in..." I stopped the spiel because he wasn't listening. He was already holding the handlebar waiting until he could jump on and ride away. "Here's the key," was all I needed for wrap-up. He grabbed it, smiling, and rode away in the same direction he had been running. I still wonder how he explained it to his parents.

In the crevices between trainings and urgencies, those quiet times on bikes and planes, the destructive behavior patterns I'd been studying took form. I wondered whether any group could devolve this way. Families? Yes, I knew that all too well. What about whole villages? Cities? Even countries?

In early May of 2005 I left for my next trip to Europe, where I'd reconnect with the European bicycle advocacy leaders. I'd somehow convinced most of the board members that not only did this connection help Thunderhead, but after three years at that relentless job, I also deserved some time off. I soon began calling it my "war studies tour."

I planned my trip, this time a full month, in two parts. The first was in Croatia, starting on the island of Veliki Brijun for the European Cyclists' Federation's (ECF) annual general meeting. We would review ECF's work from the previous year and vote on decisions for the future, much like they'd done in Madrid the year before. This time, as an official member, I could participate from the start.

My job was so all-consuming that I hadn't time to study up on Croatia before I went. I only knew vaguely that they had been part of Yugoslavia and had regained their autonomy through a war that had ended less than ten years before. I made my travel plans with trepidation. It's one thing to speak over the phone with clashing individuals, jot notes, and diagram behaviors in the safety of my home office. It's quite another to step into a place where the inhabitants had killed each other.

I knew one Croatian. I'd met Darinka the year before at the ECF meeting in Spain. We'd connected early on, laughing at the same unusual things. Her intensity and knack for finding humor everywhere was accentuated by her slight build and laughing eyes. Darinka was the director of the Croatian bicycle advocacy organization and the main organizer of the ECF meeting, so I emailed her with a few travel questions. She responded immediately with an invitation to follow her and her husband back to Zagreb after the meeting to stay with them and see a bit more of their country. Of course I accepted.

I flew to Trieste, Italy. That evening I strolled along the narrow, meandering streets to the waterfront where fishermen tinkered with their boats and gear, easing myself into my new, temporary freedom. After a restful night in Trieste, I gathered my things along with my courage and trudged to the bus station. Next stop War Zone. The first bus would take me into Slovenia, another country that had broken free with the splintering of Yugoslavia. Somewhere in that strange place I would find another bus to Pula, Croatia where I'd catch a ferry to the island. Would there still be tanks? Would I see rubble piles instead of buildings?

At least the bus was comfortable and the scenery distracting as we climbed into the hills above Trieste for a sweeping view of the coast. I pressed my face against the window to see as far south as I could to the line between Italy and Slovenia. The blue ripples of the Mediterranean showed no crease. The dark green of the lush hills and the sharp cliff faces offered no sign of the border. We left the coast to wind along narrow roads through thick forests and lively villages until the border appeared. There was no harsh line or wall differentiating countries, only a jumble of buildings connected by roofs over the road, all covered in peeling grey paint and signs in various languages. A few sleepy officers stepped briefly onto the bus to glance from afar at our passports before waving us through. The hills, forests, villages, and sunshine continued.

It was still morning when the bus dropped me off at an isolated bus depot with half a dozen rows of bus stops and a small station building overlooking a small town. There were no tanks, no piles of rubble. Tall grey apartment buildings in the distance were surrounded by red-roofed white houses, a mix of old and new. Waves of bus riders ebbed and flowed, chaos then quiet. I was taking pictures of puzzling English graffiti inside a bus shelter when my bus to Pula arrived. So far, the war zone wasn't so bad.

My Bike Hunt helpers in Pula sent me into the hills above the small, ancient city, past an enormous Roman amphitheatre that first towered over me, but as I climbed, I could peer down over the rim and through its arched openings. Tourists meandered over the stone seats and around the field where I imagined gladiators had once wrestled lions. Still climbing, I caught vistas between the white-washed and grey-stone, multi-storied houses down to the sea and tried to guess which of the Brijuni Islands was the one I'd soon be heading to.

Neither of the two bike shops my helpers sent me to were any help. The staff treated me much like staff in too many American bike shops, a behavior I'd continually had to train my bike shop employees out of. As soon as they realized I wasn't going to spend big money, they ignored me. Outside of the second bike shop, I stopped a middle-aged man with a weathered face dressed in dusty blue overalls. Between his few English words and my pantomime he understood and pointed me into a neighborhood where a man tinkered with bikes and cars. On the way there, three teenagers passed me. One spoke English and translated for the others. The other two started talking rapidly, obviously trying to convince him of something.

"How much will you pay?" he asked.

"Well," I said, trying to keep my options open, "I'll have to see the bike first, but if it's a good one, maybe 150 or 200 kuna." I was shooting for twenty-five to thirty-five dollars.

He translated to the others who shoved and prodded him. Finally, he turned back to me. "Okay," he said, "follow us."

I followed them to where he lived, an apartment in an antiquated building. They left me in a passageway that led to an inner courtyard, but soon returned with the bike—a metallic-blue mountain bike with all the basic parts in place, except someone had been messing with the headset, the front steering bearings. The kid wanted two hundred kuna or about thirty-five dollars. I pointed at the headset and complained I'd have to fix it. In the end, I got the bike for just under thirty dollars, hopped on and passed right by the bike shops, stopping instead at a car repair shop near the bus station. Just as in the United States, the car repair folks turned out to be much nicer than the bike shop jerks. They lent me all the tools I needed to give the bike a full-tune up and even rebuild and grease the headset. Next stop was the ferry and as I rode, enjoying the bike's solid ride and sturdy parts, I named him George—a good name for a solid guy.

As George and I glided onto the waterfront, I tried to pick out the ferry from all the fishing boats crowding the dock. Storm clouds arching over the sky from the north sharpened the sun's rays so the graceful hulls and masts seemed to surge from the darkening water. I was taking a photo when I heard my name. Looking back around, I found a small group of the European bicycle advocates seated with beers and smiles at an outside table. Best sight I'd seen all day. By the time the next ferry was due to leave, we'd reeled in several more of our group from our comfortable vantage point.

We took over the largest island of the bunch, Veliki Brijun, which had once been Josip Broz Tito's official summer base of operations when he ruled Yugoslavia. Leaders of bicycle advocacy organizations from nearly every European country attended. Fortunately for me, the chosen language for these meetings is English, though I could follow along a bit in separate discussions with the French, Germans, and especially the Scandinavians.

We stayed in the hotel where Tito had conducted his business—a stocky, four-story Soviet-era beige block that commanded the island's harbor. The meeting room was on the ground floor with a view of the sea. Darinka had reserved Tito's upper-story personal suite from which she and her helpers coordinated everything. This turned into the party room each night as we'd unwind after the day's work, enjoy the beer that Darinka and her team had stockpiled, and take turns out on the balcony pretending we were Tito welcoming dignitaries arriving at the dock.

On the first evening, some of us pedaled off to explore the island, past Roman ruins, military posts, villas, and signs to various places, some in English, some in Croatian. One included the words safari and park. The other riders were trying to get to the opposite side of the island before dinner so I left the group to go explore this safari park alone. I came to a huge wooden gate that reminded me of the movie *Jurassic Park*. The latch opened. Of course I went in. Strange buffalo-like creatures stared at me from a grassy slope as the enormous gate boomed shut behind me.

The park was so big, I couldn't see the far wall, so I coasted down to the left where tawny antelope-like creatures and zebras grazed. Beyond them past the seaside wall and low, wind-sculpted trees, the sea stretched to the mainland where Pula's red and white buildings climbed the slopes I'd climbed that morning. Coasting down to a path near the zebras I looked back to my left and saw enclosures amidst thick trees. Had to check that out. The zebras followed along on my right. As I neared the first, the biggest zebra stepped onto the path in front of me, flaring his nostrils. I stopped, but he didn't, slowly walking at me. I swiveled George around and hightailed it back to the gate and dinner, glad I wasn't someone else's dinner. I learned from a local that the zebra had been protecting the elephants. All the animals had been gifts to Tito from visiting dignitaries.

From my travel guide, local colleagues, and the island's museum I learned a bit about Tito and how he had held the volatile pieces of Yugoslavia together, warding off the demands of the Soviets. While Tito's country had aligned itself with the Soviet bloc, his charm and leadership skills kept their most destructive demands at bay, making Yugoslavia one of the most free-minded communist countries during his reign. Even though he was a dictator, my colleagues from the former Yugoslav states said he was actually loved by most. He could flatter other dictators as he kept them from manipulating him and harming his people.

I pondered a huge photo of Tito in the museum. Unlike leaders who share their leadership and work with the people they serve, dictators have no leeway, no room for correction if they make the slightest mistake. The brittleness of dictatorship, even one as successful as Tito's, became painfully clear when Tito died in 1980 and his country fell apart soon after. Too many bicycle advocacy organizations were heading down the same treacherous path.

This played out during the meeting. A discussion of membership fees incited accusations that an organization in a neighboring country was not paying its dues to ECF. A discussion of the next year's meeting brought insults toward the current hosts. These spikes of bitterness were much more piercing than those I'd seen at the meeting the year before in Spain—predictable jabs from the French toward the British, the Germans taking the brunt of most others. These were different. These were meant to hurt.

Each night in Tito's room, without the structure of the meeting to prevent an all-out clash, this tension rose. I have to admit that this tension intensified the fun of each night's party. Every joke or story that didn't end in a fight was doubly applauded. Small groups discussed bicycle advocacy topics to an extreme in order to ward off potential offenses.

During one encounter in Tito's room, one of the Slovenians made a snide remark about the Croatians and the room erupted into a shouting match with accusations that the Croatians had kept the war going, countered with bitter claims that the Slovenians had left the border unprotected. These were bicycle advocates, the same people who convinced their officials that cyclists had rights. Bicycle advocacy should know no borders and yet in that strange room, on that strange island, I learned that sometimes it does.

On the last day, the day the leader of the Serbian bicycle advocacy organization arrived, I walked with him to Tito's room after the meeting, knowing he would not receive a warm welcome.

He's a fairly tall man with a sorrowful face framed in grey whiskers, a face I like to try to make laugh. I was glad to be there with him, at his side as that cold wave of stares hit him and he turned and left the room. I stayed, studying the faces that had banished him, trying to decipher the tangled web of human behavior that can shun an individual and tear a country into twenty-three million sharp pieces.

Darinka's husband, Damir, drove their car from Pula east to Zagreb. Darinka and their teenage daughter Tamina took the backseat leaving the front seat to me. So many questions were swirling around in my head I couldn't keep them contained. Damir did his best to explain. As that five hour drive took us east away from the coast, into steep, forested mountains and down into low rolling hills to Zagreb, Damir's explanations changed from quick dates of battles and invasions to personal stories of how the war had hit the three of them. Darinka and Tamina, quiet at first, began offering details from the backseat. And they were laughing. That's what struck me the most. This family had kept its humanity through the gunfire, bombs, and air raids.

Darinka described days in their fourth-story apartment when she was pregnant with Tamina. Each time the air-raid sirens would sound she'd have to drop everything and run downstairs to the bomb shelter. She couldn't get anything done and running down those stairs in the last months of pregnancy strained her muscles and exhausted her. Tamina jabbed her in the ribs, teasing her for whining. Darinka pretended she was going to strangle her.

Darinka told another story, again in the apartment with infant Tamina, watching out the window as a Serbian sniper fired from across the street into the apartment next door. Again, her point was not the terror of it, rather the frustration of trying to live amidst chaos.

Their national pride showed in details of borders secured and the recognition of Croatia by the European Union. Croatia was not a new country. It had held a tenuous statehood until the invasions of the Middle Ages. Through their car windows these three welcomed me to their country they had so recently regained.

I found out why I hadn't seen any signs of the war, at least not on the ground. Most of it had been fought in eastern Croatia in a region called Slavonia. Zagreb was on the western front and as we entered the city, I gawked out the window at the broken buildings and bullet holes that pockmarked walls. While these disturbing sights caught my attention, most of the city's buildings, streets, and parks had survived unscathed.

During the three and a half days I spent with her family, Darinka gave me the bike advocacy tour of the city through sprawling outer areas with wide streets and wide paths into the narrow, busy maze of the picturesque downtown. Some of the bike paths were a bit rough and not exactly up to the standard of other cities, but what amazed me was the policy that had caused them. In those chaotic years of new government, Darinka, my clever bicycle advocacy friend, had found a way to slip a policy requiring all streets to include bikeways into a bloated land-use and housing bill.

We visited with local advocates and artists who were working for her organization, and engaged in debates at local bars about what could be accomplished next for bicycling in Croatia. The war fell into the backdrop where it belonged, replaced by an eagerness to create a better place. The war had fed this eagerness and their resulting bicycle advocacy victories. War feeding bicycle advocacy—what was I supposed to do with that?

On my last afternoon, Darinka joined me for George's giveaway. As we pedaled downtown and into an open square of mingling crowds surrounded by ornate buildings, I warned Darinka that sometimes the giveaway can be quite difficult, though I had no idea what we were in for. After nearly two hours of Darinka giving the spiel in Croatian to countless people as I played her sidekick showcasing George, we both slumped onto the edge of a fountain to regroup. Everyone we had approached was either too busy or already had a bicycle. We had just decided to make another full circle of the square when we both spotted the same man.

"That's him," I said.

"That is definitely him," she said as we walked toward him as casually as possible.

His sadness showed in his slow stride and slouched shoulders. I guessed he was in his forties, a worker with blue carpenter's pants and short, dusty blond hair. He had sauntered out of the crowd on the edge of the square and was slowly making his way to the other side. Darinka caught his attention and began the spiel. He listened intently, looking slightly down at her. When she was done, he glanced over at me and George, then back to Darinka to ask careful questions. She started getting excited, explaining and pointing at George then pointing at him, showing him the bike would be all his. That's when his face lit up and I swear he grew several inches as he turned to gaze at George. I pushed George into his hands and he pulled him close. Darinka went on talking as I fumbled for the key. I had to nudge him to pull his attention away from the bike and hand him the key, pointing to the lock. He took it as his face spread into joy and a tear formed in his eye. He sucked in some air and spoke to Darinka before throwing his leg over the bike and pedaling away. We both watched him disappear into the crowd and then Darinka sprang into a wild twirling dance around me.

"That was incredible!" she shouted, jumping and dancing in a circle so I had to keep turning to see her. "He told me his bike had been stolen weeks ago and he'd been walking for hours each day to and from work because he had no money for another bike. We just changed that man's life!"

Watching the effect of the Bike Hunt giveaway through Darinka's reaction, laughing and exclaiming along with her in the middle of that city of survivors, I could step back and see it, see why the Bike Hunt had become so essential to me.

The next day I flew to Sweden to enjoy a few days with my adopted family, then landed in Dublin on a drizzly evening about a week before ECF's bicycle conference. I had planned the whole next day for the Bike Hunt so I could find an appropriate bike for my planned cycle tour to Northern Ireland. I was staying at a hostel with endless dorms of wall-to-wall bunk beds, throbbing with shouting teenagers. I knew I could get a bed there a third night, but let's just say I hoped the hunt would lead me to a bike in one day.

I set out from the hostel first thing that next morning. The nervous man at the front counter had suggested that I start at the tourist office a few blocks away before a new swarm of backpack-clad teenagers engulfed him. It was 8:45 a.m. when I reached the locked glass doors of the tourist office—fifteen minutes to wait until they opened, not enough time to search the area for a bike. So I propped one foot up against the building and leaned back to wait. Heck, I had all day. What was the rush?

The tourist office was midblock on a broad boulevard that was divided in the middle by a wide, landscaped median. Sculptures, fountains, and flower gardens dotted the paved and grassy areas as far as I could see in both directions. Straight ahead, a dozen workers bustled around a section of the median. I settled back to watch them, the most interesting thing around. One guy was working a jackhammer that gouged out chunks of concrete around something that obviously needed to be removed. Other workers were pulling and yanking at metal pieces the guy had already jackhammered around. A few were stacking things that had been removed.

I checked my watch, getting bored. Still ten more minutes to wait. I turned back to the workers. Jackhammer, yank, pull, stack—all vaguely interesting. I glanced to each side amusing myself with what they might be creating to go along with the rest of the median amenities. Then I wondered what had been there before. Wait a minute. They're yanking out bike racks. And they're stacking abandoned bikes on the side. I can be so damn slow sometimes.

After mentally kicking myself for a minute or two, I adjusted my attitude and strolled across the traffic lanes to the median. There were three bikes in the closest stack. Another stack farther down the median was being loaded onto a truck, possible back up. One bike stood out amongst the three—a bright white five-speed Peugeot mixtie frame that reminded me of Fifi. Her tall, narrow wheels sat askew in the frame, a pedal was missing and her seat was shredded down to the metal. It was love at first sight. She even had a rear rack, which I imagined carrying my pack on my tour. The worker with the jackhammer stopped and gave me a quick inquiring nod.

"You guys getting rid of these bikes?" I asked.

"Sure are."

"Would you mind if I took that one?"

"I would thank you for it," he said. "One less bike for us to haul off."

I grabbed her grips to wheel her away, but she wouldn't roll. After standing back to assess her most serious problems, I laid her down and stomped on her front wheel until it resembled more of a circle. I borrowed an adjustable wrench from another worker and aligned her rear wheel so it would clear the frame after I released the brake. This got her rolling with only a few rubs per rotation. Before I even left the median, I named her Precious—an attempt to make up for her abandonment and abuse.

At the tourist office, the bubbly lady marked on a city map the four bike shops she knew of, dotted in four different directions around the city. Outside the fourth, after suffering yet another snub from snotty bike-shop staff, I stood on the sidewalk without a clue what to do next. I needed specialty bike tools to straighten her rims, adjust her brakes, and repack her bearings that had lost all their grease through countless rainy days. I also needed a used seat and pedal because I couldn't afford to buy new ones. Of course I expected to pay, but I wasn't going to pay for labor I could do myself or parts I didn't need. It was just past noon, three hours wasted pushing Precious to all corners of Dublin. In my dismay, I'd forgotten the Bike Hunt rule that discovery of the community is the main goal.

I'd learned that Dublin bike shops are as bad as any in the world. I'd seen the touristy parts of the old city with its narrow, cobbled streets and stout stone cathedrals. I'd crossed the river on a pretty, bowed pedestrian bridge. And I'd walked along the sidewalk of an endless speedway that led into the suburbs. I was standing on that bleak sidewalk in front of the last bike shop when my next helper surprised me. He'd been in the bike shop when I'd told my story.

"These guys are jerks," he said as he stepped out of the shop.

"I only come here because it's close to where I live. I'll tell you where you need to go."

I grabbed for my already worn city map and hurriedly opened it for him.

"It's right in the middle of the old city, but you'd never find it on your own."

I groaned. Back to where I'd started three hours ago.

"Don't worry, this guy will help you. I guarantee it."

And he was right. Kieran's shop was in a deep, narrow basement off an old-town cobbled street. I only found it by the pub sign above it that my last helper had described. As I started down the stone steps, my eyes adjusted slowly through stacks of bikes that flowed onto the steps from the depths below. When I called out "hello," I had no idea what to expect. Kieran, a wiry, middle-aged man with ruffled, sandy hair, popped out of the shadow to meet me halfway up the stairs. His slight frame was draped in grease-stained coveralls that may have once been blue.

"Hello," he said with genuine enthusiasm. "How can I help you?"

I told my long story for the fifth time that day, including, as always, that I'd been a bike shop owner for thirteen years and knew how to repair bikes and care for tools.

"Well, bring her down!" He actually said "her."

I spent the rest of the day in a bicycle-sized space between shoulder-high stacks of bikes that Kieran cleared for me at the back of his basement bike shop. As I worked, I watched in wonder as he helped an endless stream of customers. These were not his bikes. They were customers' bikes which he had fixed and then carefully stacked on their sides. The customers didn't only come to pick up bikes. Many brought more to be fixed, so the stacks never diminished. All the while, Kieran worked feverishly to keep up with the steady flow of flats, broken chains, and home repairs that needed redoing.

Later that afternoon, another man came to help. Rather than taking the chance to head out into the daylight for a break, Kieran joined me in the back to find out how Precious and I were doing. I asked him how he could possibly keep up with such demand and he shook his head like he had no choice. We also talked about the upcoming Velo-city conference, which he was planning to attend. I promised to lend a hand as soon as Precious was tour-ready, but by the time I'd straightened and trued her wheels, repacked all her bearings, installed a nice used seat and pair of pedals, it was nearly seven o'clock, well past his closing time. I apologized profusely for not being of help and then asked how much I owed for all the shop time and used parts.

"Nothing. 'Twas me pleasure to help you get ready for your cycle tour."

"No, no, no," I said, holding my ground. "I'm at least going to pay since I couldn't help."

"I'm sorry, but I don't want your money." This guy was stubborn.

"Okay," I said, as I figured out a solution, "Can I work for you tomorrow?"

I could tell he was fighting his enthusiasm before he turned away to hide it. "Well," he said, "I suppose that'd be a good idea. Could maybe find some time to work on me presentation for Velo-city."

Overhearing conversations that afternoon, I had learned that Kieran was one of Dublin's most committed bicycle advocates. Whenever he could break away from his shop, he would offer his help to bicycle projects and events. I was thrilled I could help.

That next day, I must have fixed forty bikes by five o'clock—mostly flat repairs, brake adjustments, and wheel trues, as well as diagnosed dozens of more complicated repairs to be noted and left for Kieran. The steady stream had barely let up, but I wanted to start pedaling, at least get outside the city on my first-ever cycle tour. I could tell Kieran was pleased with the help I'd given, even if I couldn't see the slightest dent in his workload. He followed me up onto the street to send me off with well wishes.

I'd left most of my stuff in a locker at the hostel. Precious's rear rack held my small pack perfectly. I found the road that led north out of the city, picking my way along its shoulderless edge as rush-hour traffic sped by. It was late evening before I turned onto the quiet coast road and finally found a bed and breakfast for the night.

For the next four days I followed the route I'd sketched along the coast into Northern Ireland, then back west and south along small inland roads to Dublin. I had a few flashes as to why some people are so enthused about cycle touring—climbing to the top of a long hill to find a breathtaking vista across farmlands dotted with cottages to the white-capped Irish Sea or the ease of putting my foot down to take in a cluster of thatch-roofed houses along a winding road lined by mossy stone walls. But for the most part I wondered why people chose cycle touring over hitchhiking or train travel with a bike.

I hadn't bothered to buy a travel guide because I'd been there before, back in 1982, on a fun trip around the southwest with my mom at the start of one of my long European adventures. That experience did not prepare me for the north. I knew there had been a war, wasn't even sure if it was over. But this was quaint Ireland, the place where local people had entertained my mother with jokes and stories that made her shriek with laughter.

Shortly after passing the deserted guard house at the border I began seeing eerie watchtowers on the rounded tops of nearby hills where sheep grazed on the grassy slopes. A monumental cross along the roadside displayed a plaque with biblical quotes alluding to peace and forgiveness. And billboards and murals shouted demands and claims against the British:

Demilitarise Now, the British cancerous spy posts
Caution Radiation Area (image of skull and crossbones)
Ireland unfree shall never be at peace
Years from now they will ask you where you were when your comrades were dying on hungerstrike. Shall you say you were with us or shall you say you were conforming to the very system that drove us to our deaths?

A couple who owned a B&B where I'd stayed south of the border said the British police had just watched from the towers as the IRA soldiers harassed citizens. On a trip to the north with their small children, the IRA soldiers at the border had pulled them out of their car and intimidated them at gunpoint because of their southern license plates.

In the tourist office in Newry, a woman in her late forties pulled me aside to ask me to fill out a tourist survey. I ended up getting more from her than she did from me. She was a Protestant from Belfast and still remembered when all "was grand," when no one worried whether another was Catholic or Protestant. As a young girl, they'd had Catholic neighbors who she adored. Then, when she was about ten years old, everything changed. Catholic and Protestant friends murdered each other. Everyone lived in fear of people they'd known all their lives.

Pedaling west and then south, the billboards, murals, and random graffiti continued touting the IRA in big block letters of green, white, and orange with nasty slogans and claims against the British and more warnings of "Radiation Danger." Some were handmade signs with peeling paint. Others were overgrown with weeds.

In a pub where I'd dashed in to escape a downpour, the well-dressed but tough bartender laughed when I asked her about the radiation signs.

"Those are just politics," she said.

I nodded like I understood, though I was not sure why she had used the term "politics." She explained that the signs referred to the British barracks in town and that the soldiers who still had to work there knew they weren't welcome, only patrolled the town for drunk drivers and such. She said that everyone knew there wasn't really any radiation danger. When I asked if there were still conflicts between British and IRA soldiers, she shook her head saying they weren't active anymore. I guessed they were as tired as their signs.

As Precious and I pedaled away from that pub, I wondered what had happened to the initial intention of the campaign. Obviously the IRA wanted Great Britain out, but their own lies and violence soon equaled those of the British. People living there could not distinguish the two and brushed them both off as "politics."

The signs had become jokes, but at the time they were painted, the IRA leaders believed their messages would build an army to kick the British out. I thought of all the sensationalism I'd encountered in the bicycle advocacy movement—claims that cars were murder machines, that unsupportive politicians and officials were killing people. We'd have to be vigilant to prevent the decay I saw eating away at Northern Ireland.

On the last day of that trip, I stepped out of the cheap hotel in Dublin, which I'd chosen over the hostel for the four days of the conference, with Precious by my side. This would be our last day together. I'd planned several hours to find the very best home for her. I couldn't move. None of the people passing by were worthy of her. I looked down at her graceful white frame, her delicate chrome fenders that had warded off so much rain, her rack that had carried my things, and tears came to my eyes. Okay, I said to myself, this is wrong. I'm not supposed to get attached to my Bike Hunt bikes. Someone in this city needs Precious. Pull yourself together.

Lifting my head, I composed myself and started down the sidewalk, adoring the smooth clicking of Precious' freewheel. It took me ten blocks before I gathered enough nerve to ask a young woman. Thankfully she didn't want a bike at that moment. I suppose I could have guessed by her high heels and that she'd just rushed out of a fancy dress shop carrying an armload of dresses in delicate wrapping. I vowed that next time I'd ask someone who appeared to actually want a bike. A cordial homeless man said he'd love to take her, but he needed to catch a bus out of town and had no place to put her. Okay, that set me on track.

After a few more blocks I rounded a corner and spotted her. She was all alone, her back to me, peering into a shop window. Her two grocery bags pulling her shoulders down added to her overall melancholy.

"Excuse me," I said to her back.

"Yes?" she said in the sweetest voice as she turned to look up at me with her kind face framed in dark wavy hair.

"I'm looking for a good home for this wonderful bicycle and

thought I'd ask if you needed one."

"Me?" she said, rather shocked as she admired Precious. "Oh dear, no. I haven't ridden a bicycle in thirty years!"

I didn't let this discourage me. Precious deserved such a kind owner and I wasn't going to back down easily. She listened to my story, making sounds of surprise and wonder as I told about the adventure Precious and I had had together, how I'd found her and how we'd been inseparable for ten days of bike tour and conference.

"I named her Precious to help her get over being abandoned. And she really is precious."

"Oh, I can see that she is a precious bike," she said.

"Here," I said, "put down your bags and try standing over her."

"You know," she said as she stood straddling Precious, her hands on the grips, "I could start in the park near my house. Oh, I bet I could find that woman who organizes weekend rides in my neighborhood. She and the others can help me learn how to ride again. Once I learn, I can do my shopping on her."

Precious had her new home and the tears that pushed at my eyes were there for a different reason than earlier that morning. I helped her step back over Precious and then showed her how to prop one bag on her rear rack and hang the other on the handlebar to make her walk home easy.

I savored the sight as they made their way down the sidewalk before turning back to my travel plans and my long journey home. At least the Bike Hunt still made sense.

7
Clinging

In early June 2005, soon after my return from my trip to Croatia, Sweden, and Ireland, the thrill of the adventure still mixed with jetlag, the phone rang. In the midst of catching up on emails, I dragged my hand from the keyboard to answer and forgot to brace myself.

"I resign." His voice was like a gunshot at my ear.

I had to fight to reenter the bizarre world where this board chair lurked. Nearly two years had passed since he'd threatened to resign over my work plan formatting. This call was particularly strange since I'd been away and had offered little if anything for him to attack. I slowed my panicked breathing, forced the air to the very bottom of my lungs and carefully released my response.

"That's too bad," I said. "But I suppose you've made up your mind. I'll let the rest of the board members know as soon as I receive your resignation in writing. Email will work fine." I hung up.

Weeks later, I was still waiting for that email. I knew that without it in writing, he could change his mind and deny resigning. It never came.

During a conference call board meeting in July, a new board member proposed that the organization be downsized, run only by volunteers, no staff, as it had been eight years before when it was founded. Classic renter's syndrome, tear down the current structure. The board chair offered ideas for making this happen. Fortunately, these comments didn't appear in the minutes. The secretary and other board members brushed them aside as nonsense.

Soon after that meeting a woman I trusted from the national organization the board chair wanted us to merge with, called to ask me about the stability of Thunderhead. I skirted the question by telling her about our successful trainings.

An America Bikes board meeting was scheduled at the end of July—the board chair and I still served on its board—in Minneapolis on the first morning of a trails conference, a welcome break from D.C. for the board members who worked there.

By July 2005, the America Bikes board was as worn out as our watered-down platform. The transportation bill was on the brink of passage by Congress. All we'd get to celebrate was the addition of a new, underfunded Safe Routes to Schools program and the preservation of bicycle and pedestrian funding that had been in the previous law. Gone was our new policy that would have required all new transportation projects to include provisions for bicyclists and pedestrians. Gone was our requirement for states to invest in bicycle and pedestrian safety improvements in correlation to the number of deaths. Gone was any increase in funding for bicycle transportation provisions. And overarching it all was billions of dollars in new funding to go into widening roads, adding traffic lanes, and creating new speedways—all deadly to cyclists. Our press releases boasted about the school program and ignored the losses.

As usual, I'd built in enough time for a Bike Hunt, arriving in Minneapolis-St. Paul the afternoon before the meeting. I followed directions south of downtown to a bicycle co-op bustling with customers and mechanics. A chiseled young man with messy blond hair pointed to a spacious, well-lit room in back with four neat lines of yet-to-be refurbished used bikes and a repair area at the rear. As soon as I walked in, I spotted her. She could have been Precious' sister, the one who never suffered abuse and abandonment. Just like Precious, she was a bright white Peugeot with a mixtie frame, fenders, and rear rack. Unlike Precious, she had ten speeds instead of five. Besides a much easier life, this was pretty much their only difference. After the young man heard my story about the Bike Hunt, he told me I could have her for twenty-five dollars. I named her Louise, a good name for the prim and proper sister of poor, battered Precious.

Strangely, I also noticed another bike with a tall frame that would have fit the board chair well, then focused back on Louise. After using the co-op's tools to give her a quick tune up, I rode Louise the long way back to the conference center, picking our way through the southern industrial area then along residential streets lined with colorful, ornate houses to downtown.

The next day dragged through the tedious, frustrating America Bikes board meeting followed by too many sessions about trails. Throughout the meeting, as usual, the board chair interrupted me anytime I spoke. During a break, I overheard him telling another board member not to pay attention to what I had said, that I had no idea what was actually going on.

By the time the last session ended, I was itching for a ride. Instead of heading out the door and jumping on Louise to ride wherever I liked, I found the board chair and told him about that tall-framed bike at the co-op. Part of me wanted to berate him for his disrespect. The other part, the part that simply wanted peace, won out. I actually went with him to get the bike, fixed it, and rode with him back to town. He seemed pleased with the bike.

The other result of this Bike Hunt olive branch was that I had to take the board chair along for the giveaway the next day. In contrast to sharing the giveaway with Darinka, he kept asking how much longer we'd have to look for recipients, kept pointing at groups of people obviously not interested in a bike. He wanted to get it over with, didn't get the point even though the scraggly older gentleman he found for his bike along an inner city trail was thrilled to receive it. I did my best to ignore his impatience as I continued on to find Louise a great home.

At another park along the same trail I spotted a family of four sitting in the grass. I guessed they were Muslim from the women's head scarves and long dresses and hesitated because Muslim women are sometimes not allowed to ride bicycles. After they listened politely to my spiel, the teenage girl stood up from the grass, glancing carefully at one and then the other parent, before asking me if it could be her bike.

"Of course," I said. "This bike would be perfect for you."

"Can I have it?" she asked her parents.

By now, her father had also stood up. At first he gave her a stern look and started to speak, but he stopped himself and turned away, then walked away. Her mother watched him go and then nodded to her daughter. By the time Louise's grips were in her hands and I'd given her the key to the lock, her younger brother was climbing on the rear rack asking if he could ride it. This sibling struggle would be a slight problem for Louise in her new home. As the board chair walked silently ahead of me back to the train for the airport, I knew my own serious struggle continued.

His calls changed into interrogations. He grilled me about local organizations, about potential partners and funders, and about bicycle policies and provisions I'd encountered during my travels as if he was trying to squeeze any remaining value out of me before he could discard me. I kept my answers short.

After one of those calls, I read the Thunderhead bylaws hoping for protection, dreading what I'd find. Sure enough, they were the exact copied-and-pasted words I had found in bylaws of other organizations in crisis. They clearly set the executive director out as inferior to the board and outlined in detail the many ways to terminate this staff position, even without cause.

The next training was in Decatur, Georgia, just east of Atlanta, at the end of August 2005, with Gayle as the main trainer. The day before the training the local bicycle advocates drove me and Gayle around to gather supplies, then dropped me off at a bike co-op where they were sure I would find a bike.

As with most bike co-ops, no one was in charge, but the young man I asked showed me the piles of unfixed bikes outside that were available. At the bottom of one particularly muddy and rusty jumble a cheerful glint of yellow caught my eye. After yanking and untangling I finally released a fully intact, sunshine-yellow beach cruiser with five gears. I rolled him over to the outside patio where a dozen people were working on bikes under bright lights that anticipated the setting sun. I turned him upside down and got to work. Soon a few of the regulars, including a chubby guy with a chewed-up, greasy-grey ball cap, came over to inform me of their rules. Their bike co-op, like most others, had a goal of getting bikes to people who needed them, but operated under an unusual system where you could get a bike for a twenty-five-dollar refundable deposit. They'd fix the bike for you, paint it yellow to mark they owned it, and you'd bring it back when you were done to receive your twenty-five dollars back.

I had the darnedest time explaining that I'd prefer to work on the bike myself. Then I had to beg them to let me give the bike away. I was glad to pay the twenty-five dollars, handing over the two bills, but I wouldn't be back. They were more interested in their rules than ensuring the bike went to someone who needed it. Finally I convinced them and got back to work on the bike.

It wasn't long before the chubby guy with the cap reappeared at my side.

"You'll need this for the chain," he said, holding out a spray can of WD-40, a solvent that helps break rusted parts free, but is the opposite of a lubricant.

"That's okay," I said, "I'll find some oil instead."

But he wouldn't have any of that. To him, WD-40 was the only thing you could put on a bicycle chain. Somehow I managed to fend him off. When he came back with a can of yellow spray paint, I started to wonder if the local bike advocates had dropped me off here as a joke.

"He's already yellow!" I said, standing in front of the bike like a shield.

"But it's our bike," he said.

"No," I said as calmly as I could. "Remember, I paid you your twenty-five dollars and I will not be coming back for the money. Instead, I will find someone who really needs this bike and give him to them. That's what we just agreed to."

"But that's not our system. It's still our bike."

"No, it will be that person's bike and you get to keep the twenty-five dollars. Okay?"

"Yeah, but it's our..."

"Please, this bike is already yellow," I said, fighting the urge to ask how they expected to help people with bikes if they never relinquished ownership of them. "You can still pick him out in town and know he was once one of your bikes. Okay?"

"Okay, but..."

"Okay?"

"Well... okay."

This little volunteer-run organization had clearly forgotten its purpose and let a poorly crafted policy take over. I would have offered tips for refocusing toward their mission of helping people with bikes, but any interaction was sure to bring back that dreaded can of yellow paint.

It was dark when Sunny and I rolled off that perplexing, spot-lit patio. I had named him Sunny because each time I turned back to him after fending off that guy with the vile spray cans, he made me smile. His curvy yellow frame and fat tires were all about fun, not arguing.

The three-day training in Decatur was a welcome, if temporary, escape from the escalating threat to my job and reputation. More than forty leaders of bicycle advocacy organizations from all over the south, plus three from California, had signed up. Their interactions during breakout sessions were some of the liveliest I'd seen.

After packing up on Sunday afternoon, several bike advocates, a city official who had attended, and Gayle came along on Sunny's giveaway. This was southern hospitality where everyone shares their joys and hardships. We strolled through Decatur's charming downtown with trees and flowerbeds accentuating cafes and locally-owned shops in a mix of new and historic buildings. The streets were so narrowed that the cars moved at walking speed. Cyclists of all ages wove nonchalantly among the cars. The people in the park and strolling along the broad sidewalks had a lazy, contented look about them. Most were in pairs or family groups, not candidates for Sunny.

After half an hour, I spotted a woman sitting alone in the sun at a sidewalk cafe across the street—styled strawberry-blond hair, not fat, but not fit—sinking into the book she held in her lap. I stopped, but the group kept walking, engaged in a discussion with the city official about Decatur's bicycle and pedestrian improvements. I had to shout for them to stop and come back to the street corner where I stood with Sunny, watching the woman all the while to make sure she hadn't heard me. I pointed and they all saw her, smiling and nudging me, whispering for me to go get her. It was all I could do not to laugh.

Once I'd gathered myself, I crossed the street with Sunny and worked my way through the pedestrians to the low metal fence that surrounded the tables. Her table butted up against the fence so it was easy for me to approach her without appearing weird.

"Excuse me," I said as casually as I could. "I wondered if you might be able to help me." I must have chosen the southern hospitality angle subconsciously.

"Yes, of course," she said, slowly lifting her eyes from her book. "How can I help you?"

I'd connected. After she heard my spiel, she sat up and peered over the fence at Sunny—eyes wide, brows high, knuckles white as she gripped the fence.

"It's such a lovely bicycle. Are you sure you'd want to give it to me? I haven't ridden in such a long time. Do you think this would be a good bike for me to start bicycling again? I have no place to put it now..."

I had to interrupt her to show her that Sunny had a lock, offering her the key, so she could easily lock him to the fence while she finished what she was doing. She released her grip on the fence and let me drop the key into her outstretched palm. Deal sealed. She thanked me, or maybe she thanked the key because she didn't look up. I left her to enjoy the moment.

When I turned around, my peanut gallery was clapping. I had to make exaggerated hand signals for them to stop, keeping my hands within the frame of my body so she wouldn't see. They stopped clapping but remained in a spectator row, smiling and commenting to each other. I walked as fast as I could back to them, glancing back only once to see that she had not yet looked up, and ushered them quickly out of her view.

From Decatur, I flew to D.C. for some meetings, then to Chicago for the next America Bikes board meeting because my fellow board members liked to hold our meetings away from D.C. No time for a Bike Hunt. Three cities in a week.

Back at my home office, I caught up with members and projects through September, with only one trip to Las Vegas for the annual Interbike trade show, until I could no longer avoid preparing for the annual board meeting at the board chair's house in Chicago in October. There was one hopeful item on the agenda—he had held the top seat as chair of the board for nine years, since Thunderhead was founded, and had finally offered to step down, but not off the board. I tried to convince myself that this would make a difference.

I asked for discussions of all of our programs to be part of the agenda—campaign planning trainings, the federal transportation bill, bicycle statistics, and of course the 50/50 Project—along with staff roles (by then I had three part-timers helping with the 50/50 effort, bike statistics, trainings, and member resources). I did this knowing that the new board member, now joined by another, would again propose downsizing the organization back to all-volunteer-run, removing these programs and any need for staff, including me.

I arrived in Chicago the afternoon before the full-day meeting, secured a bed at a hostel between downtown and Wrigley Field, then set out on the hunt. The young woman at the hostel desk suggested I go to a bike shop at the end of a long bus ride north. Under cloudy skies promising rain, the bus pulled up just before five. As the bus crawled along in rush hour traffic, I wondered if the shop would stay open until six. We reached the end of the block after ten agonizing minutes. At that rate I would be lucky to reach the bike shop by the next day. After three more snail-paced blocks I spotted a lineup of used bikes outside a thrift store and sprang out the bus doors.

I picked Jim Lucas out of the line of bikes. He was a beautifully preserved 1950s black Raleigh three-speed, the sort of bike you'd see British factory workers riding in old movies. The name "Jim Lucas" had been engraved in the top tube of the frame, so he was easy to name. Clearly, bike owner Jim Lucas had cared deeply for bike Jim Lucas. The elderly woman at the counter in the back worked her way through the narrow slots between clothes racks and furniture to unlock the cable and take my two twenty-dollar bills. At the gas station a block away, all I had to do was air up his tires and take a wrench to his axle nuts. He was ready to ride.

The next morning, pedaling to the meeting through quiet residential neighborhoods in the chilly morning mist, I went over the agenda, making sure I'd brought all the supporting items and documents, running through likely threats—the merger, the all-volunteer proposal—and how I'd respond to protect myself, my staff, the organization, when suddenly the air couldn't reach my lungs. Stars popped around me. I stopped on the edge of the street to rest my forehead on my arms folded across Jim Lucas' handlebar. I focused on filling my lungs, once, twice, and a third time, then set out pedaling again. A glance at my watch quickened my pedal strokes as I told myself it was just another meeting.

Turning a corner my rhythm skipped. In the middle of the street a man in an electric wheelchair was desperately jabbing at the power lever. All the chair would do was lurch forward, then stop again. The guy was about my age of forty-one, a bit overweight, with dark hair and beard. It didn't look like he could move his legs, and only one arm could move with much accuracy as he exclaimed his frustration to me. I helped him roll the chair out of the middle of the street—me pushing hard from behind because it was stuck in gear, him swinging forward like the motion of a swing. Together we got him to a spot that cars could pass safely. Studying the gearbox and switch, I found where it was jammed—a junction held together by a hex Allen screw. But I didn't have the right Allen wrench with me.

I promised I would return and set off as fast as I could, arriving at the board chair's patchwork alley house with only this mission in mind. That guy and his broken-down wheelchair had defused my panic. The husband of the board member from Seattle went back to fix the wheelchair as I settled into the long, inescapable meeting. The board chair was shifted to a regular board position and the woman from Seattle who I respected and trusted became the new chair. My staff and I emerged from the meeting with our jobs intact, though our raises had been deferred until the next face-to-face board meeting in February in D.C.

Dusk had slipped into darkness, a misty rain falling, when I finally pedaled away, feeling lighter with each pedal stroke. In the shadow of a featureless concrete building across from Wrigley Field, I let Jim Lucas coast up onto the sidewalk and to a stop. The stadium spotlights and street lamps painted the planes of concrete and pavement yellowy white, split by sharp blue-grey shadows, all glossed by the rain. Only a few cars passed as I delighted in the stark setting. For that moment, I believed the danger had passed. I believed I could return to my job as executive director of the Thunderhead Alliance, finally spending my time helping bicycle organizations, free from the power struggle, free from threats.

I pedaled downtown the next day to give Jim Lucas away. As I turned onto Michigan Avenue, its wide expanse between skyscrapers and landscaped median forced me to choose a side. I chose the southbound side and slowed to a crawl to study the passing faces. Most of the pedestrians were in suits or fancy dresses rushing to important places. Behind this flow of people I spotted a stationary man. He was sitting on a rolled-up blanket, his smudged, bearded face watching the people pass as if he was at a tennis match. No one stopped to drop coins into his hat. His sign read simply, "Please." I liked that. No specifics, just a polite please. I used to add that word to the end of my hitchhiking signs. Still, I wanted to make sure he'd take care of Jim Lucas before committing. After rolling up to him, I could tell he didn't see me because he was so focused on the rush in front of him. I'd come from the side and was no longer moving.

"Hi," I said.

"Huh?" he said. "Geez, where did you come from?"

"Sorry to surprise you," I said, moving my eyes back to the swirling crowd for a moment to let him get used to me. "So," I began again, "what's your story?"

He sat up a bit, obviously pleased that I'd asked and scooched a bit closer to me as I leaned down across the handlebar to listen. He started by asking my name. His was A. J. Then he told me of thieves and beatings, the fear he felt each night when he tried to sleep, the vulnerability he was growing so tired of. And then, as if to balance this fear, he told me how much he still loved his girlfriend who had left him nearly a year before to fend for himself on the street. When I asked him if a bike would help, he frowned, saying he couldn't buy a bike. But when I explained further, his blue eyes brightened.

"Would you really give me that beautiful bike?" he asked.

"I would be honored to give you this beautiful bike," I said.

He stood up slowly, his eyes on Jim Lucas. I pushed him into A. J.'s hands and he swung his leg over to straddle the frame. After one quick glance at me he jumped onto the saddle and started riding in a circle, disrupting the flow of people who had to step sideways and then collide with others. A. J. no longer cared about them as he laughed and chattered about all the places he could go now, riding many more circles on the sidewalk. He coasted to a stop in front of me to give me a hug. As I walked away, he chanted my name.

A few weeks back at my home office set me on edge again as my certainty of the reprieve waned. Even as I responded to the needs of our members, I recoiled from the ring of the phone or an incoming email from a board member. No more threats surfaced, but I searched between the lines for what might be lurking.

Later that month, October 2005, I was relieved to be on another Bike Hunt, this one in San Francisco before our next training, though the hunt was the fastest yet. I went straight to the thrift store in the Mission District where I'd bought The Wedge two years before. I marched upstairs where they kept the bikes and pulled Susie Q out after my first scan. She was a deep purple girls' BMX with twenty-inch white tires. Like Jim Lucas, she was easy to name because "Susie Q" was painted on her side. After paying the twenty dollars, I rolled her across the street to an auto repair shop, aired up her tires, and she was ready to ride.

The training was an all-around success. In the afternoon of the third day, still high on the enthusiasm from attendees, I walked out onto Market Street with Susie Q for one more taste of nostalgia from my days as a San Francisco bike messenger. I pedaled hard and leaped the tall curb. A good dose of imagination was necessary since my messenger bikes had been full-sized cruisers and back in the 1980s, there were no bicycle facilities. This time I was riding in a bike lane passing and being passed by cyclists of all ages and styles. The local advocates had transformed their city into a place that invited anyone to ride, the sort of transformation I longed for other Thunderhead members to celebrate. But if I squinted, I could still imagine darting through that traffic chaos. As the low buildings of west Market eased into the skyscrapers of the Financial District, Susie Q and I took a high-speed right onto Second, cutting through oncoming traffic, a left onto Mission, another left back onto Market and a hard sprint to its end at the Ferry Building. I had to squint hard to remember the dark shadow of the freeway that once loomed there. In its place a park-like boulevard in sunlight was dotted with trees and people.

My joyride was over, time to find Susie Q a home. Pedaling back up Market, I spotted a mother and daughter walking together. The daughter was about eight years old, a much better size for Susie Q. After they listened to my spiel, the daughter's face lit up as her mother nodded approval. She immediately got on to ride so I had to give the key to the mother. As I walked away, she was riding circles around her mother, giggling.

A quick trip to D.C. a few weeks later for meetings and a community development conference and I was back in my home office. Winter eased along. The monthly board meetings went smoothly enough. I was able to focus on wrapping up our bicycling statistics report, work with my staff to adjust our training curriculum for the next year, and reach out to partners. I even spent some quality free time on my study of the strange group behaviors I'd been encountering.

The first month of 2006 offered a welcome diversion with another community development conference, this time in Denver. The Bike Hunt led me to a thrift shop where the scraggy guy at the counter pointed me to the back where they'd piled a bunch of bikes. On top of the pile of mass-merchant bikes was an all-steel ten-speed bike with a curved women's frame. She wasn't exactly pretty with her industrial blue paint and basic lines, but she was solid. I about strained myself lifting her off the pile. After paying ten dollars, I dubbed her The Iron Maiden.

After the conference, I took her on the bus to Boulder to see Karen, my friend from D.C. Karen had moved to Boulder for various reasons, leaving Fifi in D.C. with a mutual friend who was happy to let me borrow her. We had lots of catching up to do in one day, talking nonstop at her house and later on a bike tour of her new city at the jagged edge of the Rockies.

The bike path network was impressive and yet something bothered me about that place. Everyone looked wealthy, white and wealthy. This was no cross-section of America, more like a city-sized gated community. I flashed back to that moment in downtown Portland when that black woman in the Goodwill had laughed at my assumption that she actually lived there. As we pedaled back through downtown toward Karen's house, I wondered if I could find a home for The Iron Maiden in that fabricated city. When we passed a homeless shelter near the bus station, I rubber-necked so hard I nearly jackknifed her, then memorized the cross streets.

That evening, Karen invited some local bike advocates to her place for dinner and bike banter since I was in town. One was the woman who had gotten me my job at Thunderhead.

A moment after dinner remains clear and detailed. She and another advocate sit on the couch across from me, Karen next to me in another chair. Our laughter after the last story is dying down when that woman asks me, in a sick-joke tone, how I am getting along with the former chair. The others fight back their laughter. She can hardly restrain herself. I want to puke. I look her in the eye and answer fine, then wait, my eardrums buzzing, until Karen changes the subject.

The next morning, I headed straight to the shelter. As I pedaled up, there were a dozen guys hanging out in a tight group. I stopped in the street next to them, got their attention, gave my spiel and settled back on The Iron Maiden's seat to take in the reaction. Some laughed, others elbowed, teasing one guy that he needed a bike to lose some weight, another that he could use it to leave town. Watching the faces I was starting to wonder if I'd come up dry, when I heard a voice from below.

"I need a bike," the voice said, this time sincere.

I looked down to find lying on the sidewalk a Grizzly Adams type, complete with beard and tussled blond hair, crutches at his side. I tuned out the jeers and moved closer to hear him.

"My bike got stolen about three months ago," he continued, "and ever since, this sciatic nerve has plagued me. When I was riding that bike, I was fine, could even work. Now look at me. I'm a damned cripple."

The jeers had stopped. They were listening too.

"Wow," I said, "You definitely need a bike. But how do you know you can actually ride her?"

Rather than answer, he struggled to sit up and then get to his feet, wincing. One of the other guys helped him get his crutches. I got off The Iron Maiden and lined her up near the curb. Using his crutches, he lowered himself into the street, then handed them back to the guy who had helped. He took hold of her handlebar, slid his leg carefully through her low-curved frame and eased himself onto the saddle. The group hushed.

"Oh yeah," he said, like a mountain man astride a wild horse, "I can ride her, no problem."

"I named her The Iron Maiden," I said. "You feel her weight?"

"That's cool," he said with a daring grin as he gazed at all sides of his new ride. "That's the perfect name for her."

At this, the group erupted into hoots and applause.

February 2006 arrived too soon and with it the same dread I'd felt before that October board meeting in Chicago. The two new board members had continued pushing their proposal for an all-volunteer organization with the former chair lending his support. By then, they had added a new twist: that the organization had no business operating in Washington, D.C., at all. They asked this to be included in the agenda and the former chair agreed. The irony of holding our February board meeting in D.C. to discuss not operating in D.C. did not escape me.

Their opposition to our D.C. presence had followed my recent request to open a satellite, virtual office there. I had been traveling to D.C. frequently to attend America Bikes board meetings, meet with our partners, lobby key members of Congress, and connect with the local bicycle advocates in that area. A proper office in D.C. would help me do a better job and demonstrate our worth as a national organization. I'd started investigating these companies that offer shared office spaces for entities not based in D.C. back when the former chair was still calling for the merger. I had hoped that having our own office in D.C. would prevent that from resurfacing. Now his push for the merger had switched to his support of the all-volunteer, no-D.C. proposal. Perhaps the national organization he wanted to merge with had snubbed him. Perhaps there was no explanation for his bizarre, erratic behavior over the years. Whether his intentions were deceptive or delusional, they remained shrouded from me.

Since I'd taken the job, I'd ensured that our budget had steadily grown and we retained a net surplus of at least twenty-five thousand dollars at the end of each year, growing our reserve. Because of this, I knew that we could easily afford this D.C. office at only three hundred dollars per month. Since the office was shared, they didn't have to charge much per client. It also provided a receptionist who would answer our line "Thunderhead Alliance," meeting rooms, internet, and shared office equipment. Cheap rent for a staffed office right across from the White House with a street address of 1700 Pennsylvania—mighty slick. Still, the two new board members aggressively opposed it, emailing the rest of the board that we must instead "return to our roots."

After me, the former chair was the next to arrive at the meeting, held in the back office of the local bicycle advocacy organization. He avoided eye contact. Most of the other board members filed in loudly as they caught up with their latest activities. I did my best to join in, to be part of the group. I watched my two staff members with concern as they too tried to join in. I'd recently moved them to full-time as our third had asked to change to an occasional contract trainer position. Both these guys were of average build with dark hair, one with a tough facade helping develop 50/50 and training resources, the other a techie working on web resources and bike statistics, both sweethearts.

The new chair of the board, the woman I was counting on, would not be there. Instead, she would join the crucial part of the meeting by speakerphone. I fixated on the two staff from the local organization as they set up the speakerphone-lifeline in the middle of the table.

As the first part of the meeting on program updates ended, one of the board members dialed the phone number for the chair. Her faint voice crackling through the tiny speaker holes was like sparklers in a cave. After reviewing the budget, my staff and I were asked to leave the room. As we fidgeted around the front office, one of them asked me if I thought they could fire us all and I told him yes. Finally, we were called back in. Three faces glowed with appreciation, three kept their eyes low. The new board chair had stood up for us. We had our jobs and, miraculously, our raises. We even had the go-ahead for the D.C. virtual office.

After finishing my meal at a tense dinner with the board and staff at a nearby restaurant, I slipped out onto the sloping sidewalk of Connecticut Avenue to lean on Fifi and catch my breath, free from the threat once again. I briefly considered a ride downhill for another ritual visit to the Declaration of Independence Memorial. Since my discovery of it in November 2001, the reading of the tablet had become a masochistic ritual that I both desired and loathed. If I found I had time I would ride Fifi to the memorial, pedaling right up to the words before slumping over her handlebar to read, searching between the words for the reason why they had absolutely no connection to what I was experiencing, "....*we mutually pledge to each other our Lives, our Fortunes and our sacred Honor."* Sometimes the tablet was bathed in sunlight. Sometimes I'd wait as snowflakes swirled over the words. Other times Fifi's stem dug into my sternum as I'd grit my teeth against torrential rain pouring over me and all but washing the words away. I studied those words innumerable times, pulling at them to find how they could flow into the national bicycle advocacy movement until all I could see was stone.

This time, I pointed Fifi uphill and rode to The Asylum, the bike messenger bar in Adams Morgan. I needed to be near them, to hear camaraderie.

Back at my office, I did my best to refocus on my job, a job I adored when I was allowed to do it. After nearly four years, I still believed this was the place for me, my calling—the executive director of a national organization that served local bicycle organizations, honoring their expertise and giving them the credit they deserved. The Thunderhead board was a turnstile. Nearly all the faces changed each year, all except the former chair of course. I kept telling myself it would soon change into a sensible group who would not put up with discussions of tearing Thunderhead apart or killing it through a merger.

After that D.C. meeting, the former chair restarted his merger chant and I listened for any sign of support from other board members. It seemed he was starting from square one again and we were safe for the time being. Between board meetings I convinced myself that things were getting better, using the leaders of local bicycle organizations as my blinders, agonizing with them as they fought for bicycle initiatives and sharing their joy when they won. But they were lousy blinders. Very few of them could focus entirely on bicycle initiatives. Bizarre group behaviors, mostly from their boards of directors, sapped their energy and sometimes shut down their organizations entirely.

In March 2006, I flew to San Antonio, Texas to take part in a technical seminar for the Institute of Transportation Engineers. I was to present the concern that most streets in the United States are incomplete for bicyclists and pedestrians. I landed on a Sunday afternoon. On the bus ride from the airport, I was surprised to see some pawn shops open.

After I checked in at the motel near downtown, a woman on the street corner pointed me back along that bus route, noting the pawn shops I'd seen. I set out on the long walk with confidence, but before I reached them my watch showed fifteen minutes to five. If the pawn shops were still open, they sure wouldn't be open after five on a Sunday. I took off running over the jumbled chunks of what had once been a sidewalk, noting it for my complete streets presentation the next day. I ran up the sloped parking lot to the first pawn shop at two minutes before five and flew through the door to grab the counter like it was home base.

"Got any bikes?" was all I could manage with my remaining breath, ready to sprint out the door toward the next pawn shop if the answer was no.

Instead of answering, the slender man behind the counter chuckled and pointed his chin to the back of the shop where a full-chrome BMX bike shone among electric guitars. He had all his parts, needed adjustments, but nothing serious.

"How much?" I asked.

"Twenty," the man answered. He seemed to be enjoying my mini drama. "That would be a fun bike for you."

"Yeah it would," I said. He was made for big teenagers, the type they make fly from jumps and half-pipes.

I rolled the bike across the busy thoroughfare to a car repair shop. A mechanic stepped out from the single bay and asked if I needed help with my bike, before I could even ask. He was a middle-aged Hispanic man with a thick accent and a commanding air that showed he was the owner.

"Make yourself comfortable and I'll bring you all the tools you need," he said.

"But aren't you closing soon?"

"Closing?" he asked, as he looked at his watch. "It is getting late. But, no, don't worry, I still have some work to do on this car. Have a seat." He pointed to a line of plastic chairs outside the door to the office, right next to the sidewalk.

One of the chairs was already occupied by an ancient man. I sidled up and waited for his approving nod before I settled down into the chair next to him. "Nice bike," was all he said.

Long minutes passed. Then a quarter of an hour. After my panicked run, I had to struggle to make the shift, reminding myself to let the hunt show me this community. Finally the mechanic/owner returned with two handfuls of tools, spreading them out on the sidewalk. Soon I had a bike. I gave back the tools and thanked him for his hospitality, bid farewell to the old man who nodded again. As I leaped the curb across the old man's view, I dubbed my new ride Silver.

Silver and I explored San Antonio each morning and evening. There was a peculiar river path below street level where lots of shops had their storefronts. I could ride for blocks of only office buildings and parking garages, empty sidewalks, no restaurants or stores. But if I stopped to peer over a bridge down to river level, I'd see swarms of tourists flowing in and out of shops and sitting at restaurants. It was like the city had moved below ground to cater entirely to tourists.

On that first evening, I finally found people at street level, a crowd even. I thought I'd come across a beacon of hope, but my heart sank as I realized it was only a bus stop with a crowd of tired workers leaving the city for the evening. The next day, I found where the workers lived, way out in a valley between freeways, most of the houses not more than shacks with chickens, dogs, and children kicking up dust in the bare yards, not a part of the city.

After lunch on the last day of the conference, I rode Silver to the bus stop where I would catch the bus to the airport, looking for an appropriate recipient along those empty streets. The bus stop happened to be at the edge of a tiny, lot-sized park, unusual for that city because it actually invited locals to linger. A hotdog vendor had a long line waiting. Families were picnicking in the grass. Workers of all types, some in work pants, others in business attire, sat on the low rock wall that encircled the lawn. I soaked in the scene before starting my slow ride around the park to find Silver his new owner.

Halfway through my second lap, I spotted a man, maybe mid-thirties, wearing clean worker's pants and a new plaid shirt, who had just bought a hot dog. The way he stood holding it, not eating, just thinking, gave me my cue.

"Excuse me," I said.

"Yes?" he asked, obviously suspicious of me riding this BMX bike, a backpack on my back.

I stepped off in front of him in an effort to look a bit more normal. "I'll be catching the bus to the airport soon to fly back to Arizona where I live. I've been riding this wonderful bike I bought at a pawn shop, but now I need to find someone who can take care of him. For free, only the commitment to take care of him."

I knew I'd gotten his attention when he began asking questions, mostly so I would repeat that I was soon leaving and could very well leave that bike with him. By then, his hand had drooped to his side in his amazement and I worried he might drop the hotdog. He must have caught my glance because he set it down on the wall. With his hands free, I was able to push Silver toward him until he grabbed the grips and straddled the frame. He thanked me, then told me how this bike would add to a turning point that had happened earlier that day. After months without work, nearly losing his house, he had found a job. Now he could ride this bike and save bus money. When I told him the bike's name was Silver, he clenched his jaw.

"My daughter's name... is Silver," he said, as he turned away so I'd never know if the tears flowed. I left him like that, not turning back as the bus pulled up and I jumped on.

Back in Prescott, the demand from our members for my assistance increased even as I prepared for our next training in D.C in May. Over the years, I'd developed the groove that allowed this ever-increasing workload. Wake up, descend the stairs, make coffee, respond to urgent emails and phone calls, respond to others, check in with staff and respond to their needs, then finally after dark when the emails and calls ease, create training and program materials or prepare for the next trip, climb the stairs, collapse in bed. Do it all again the next day.

Communications from board members had become cordial, the sort of messages you get from distant relatives you're supposed to be polite to. I continued to send frequent detailed reports, anticipating their demands to prove my claims, five or six pages to show our progress. Though I hoped they would read them, their questions during meetings showed they hadn't.

I worked with them to create my first employee agreement to align with the raise to fifty thousand dollars a year that they'd approved in February in D.C., but even with four weeks vacation locked into that agreement, I had to beg for them to let me take two weeks to attend the European Cyclists' Federation annual gathering and travel a bit.

The 2006 ECF gathering at the end of May was held in Klaipeda, Lithuania. The bus driver from the airport recommended I get out in a small town along the way. Sure enough I found Sophia, a woman's-frame Soviet-era single speed with faded green paint, at a car and bike repair shop. After enjoying my friends at the meeting and along a three-day group ride down the Curonian Spit and back to Klaipeda, I gave Sophia to a lone woman walking along a housing development path carrying a heavy shopping bag. She reached into the bag and pulled out a yellow rose for me as her thanks. I spent a few days in Norway with bike advocates and a few days with my family in Sweden before rushing back to Prescott to catch back up with the ever-increasing load.

Not long after my return, an executive director of one of our member organizations called me to describe his plan to sabotage his organization because his board had hired a consultant to take over much of his responsibilities. Through careful questions, keeping him talking, I convinced him that his board had no idea how offensive this had been to him, guiding him away from revenge and toward a graceful resignation. This call was the closest I'd been to the brink of disaster with one of our members. I had become a trusted lifeline.

In Denver in July for our next training, I found Cranky when I asked the workers in the back of a thrift shop. They pointed to him in the corner, not fit for the sales floor. His bottom bracket bearings were nearly shot. I paid two dollars, then made him ridable. After the training, I gave Cranky to a man playing chess with his buddies on the 16th Street Mall.

After Denver I had three weeks in Prescott before my next trip, this one to Milwaukee, Wisconsin for another Institute of Transportation Engineers conference. Many conferences like this were exploratory. I was reaching out to engineers, the development community, health and smart-growth entities, any industry or movement that should care about bicycling, in order to release Thunderhead from its dependence on the bicycle industry. Also, the more of these events I could attend, the more chance I'd have of breaking Thunderhead away from a merger under the bike industry's thumb.

I paid for these exploratory trips myself since they were not in our budget. Through these trips, I had already won an ongoing partnership with the Centers for Disease Control at fifty thousand dollars per year to pay for our bicycling statistics project. The board seemed pleased. I had met with major developers about adding bicycle programs to their affordable housing projects, led by our member organizations, to help low-income people start bicycling. I discussed this with Fannie Mae to fund Thunderhead at one hundred thousand dollars per year. A developer in the D.C. area was ready to be our first model once the funding came through, had even driven me around to some of her properties that could qualify. My explorations were paying off, but they were costing me more than money—sometimes three trips in one month, some so short I didn't bother with a Bike Hunt.

I found Smiley in Milwaukee with the help of a porter at the engineering conference hotel, his buddy's bike. This guy never stopped smiling, thus the bike name. Smiley was a beat-up mass merchant BSO, but ridable. I gave him to a woman waiting at a bus stop who had once lived in Portland riding everywhere, but was afraid to ride here. She'd give Smiley a chance.

A few more weeks back in Prescott was all I had to prepare for our next retreat, in Madison, Wisconsin at the end of August. The threat would be there again at our board meeting prior to the retreat. Whether it was losing the organization through the merger or being fired under the next call for idealistic downsizing, the result would be the same. I was growing numb to anxiety. During the meeting I pushed programs, talking over board members gossiping about other national organizations, demanding their input should Fannie Mae or the other potential new partners fund us. Though I captured a few of their ideas on the blank papers I'd taped to the walls, I felt as though I was in a different room from them, alone.

During the bike conference that followed the retreat I rode with a group of our members to a party at a bike company based there. They were one of our top funders so I was looking forward to having some fun with them. Our main contact there greeted me with a battery of questions about Thunderhead, our members, our other funders, our programs. If he hadn't been standing right in front of me, I would have sworn he was the former chair.

Mad Lee, short for Madison Lee, was my bike for that trip, a chrome BMX bike made in China. I gave him to a twitchy young guy, just in from New York City, who had been missing a job training program because he lived too far away. With the bike he was sure he could make it.

In ten days at the end of October, I traveled back to Denver for a developers' conference, then to Philadelphia for our next training, to D.C. for meetings, and finally to Los Angeles for a community development conference. I only managed one Bike Hunt in those four trips: Birdy in Philadelphia, a blue women's-frame from the '50s. Named her Birdy for her squeak. At the bus station, I gave her to Cisco—no front teeth, no food either, big plans to paint her. Four cities in ten days was my new travel record.

That fall, the former chair again demanded a strict review of my performance, complete with a formal review committee and contracting out a financial audit that cost Thunderhead three thousand dollars. After months of filling out forms, shuffling receipts, and enduring interrogations, the committee declared my performance "very positive." All records were in order and they were pleased with the results of my work.

He called again a few days before Christmas to threaten me with his resignation. I just let him boast about how little he cared for Thunderhead, that he was only staying on the board for his national agenda, whatever that was.

Though 2006 was a tremendous year for Thunderhead—I'd brought in two hundred and fifty thousand dollars in revenue and increased our member organizations to 128—the year 2007 began in sadness. A longtime executive director of one of our member organizations had been fired by her board. She had called me several times over the past year as the situation had developed. The chair of her board didn't like her and wanted her gone. At one point he had actually fired her, but they were alone in the office and their bylaws required the whole board to vote on a termination, so she refused to leave. Gutsy. He must have finally convinced a simple majority. I only received their public announcement and had to find her personal phone number to tell her how sorry I was.

A week later, the chair of the board of another member organization called me immediately after firing their executive director, also without cause. They'd had an argument and in the chair's anger, she had fired her knowing that their bylaws gave her that power. The chair was in tears when I answered, but there was nothing I could do to help her correct her mistake. I could only coach her on steps to mop up the mess and change their bylaws to prevent it from happening again.

These two tragedies redoubled my determination to stop bad behaviors within our member organizations. My earlier concerns about ineffectiveness had now grown to encompass actions that harmed individuals and left their organizations floundering. Two unjustified firings in a matter of weeks only showed the problem had not improved. I had been stomping brushfires, but not finding or changing the source. So much wasted time, so many great leaders crushed, never to return to the bicycle movement. None of this did anything to increase bicycling. I set to work on training materials for my staff to teach them what I'd learned about responding to organization emergencies, including danger signs so they could steer leaders back to effective work before an emergency occurred. This added to my work load, but I didn't care. We had to do something to stop this dysfunction and prevent more tragedies. None of the board members seemed interested in this new project.

The Pup was my bike in Los Angeles during a smart-growth conference in February—a blue BMX bike with a wide handlebar, bought from Wolf spitting sunflower shells and pushing a shopping cart. Gave him to a skateboarder who had a hard time hiding his happiness from his cool buddies.

In D.C. in March, at our board meeting held in our satellite office next to the White House, the woman from Seattle stepped down as chair and off the board. The young advocate from New York City, the same one who had joined me on Victoria's giveaway, became chair. The former, original chair remained on the board.

At a cocktail party on Capitol Hill after lobbying with bike advocates at the Bike Summit, the same bike company representative who had harangued me in Madison told me it was time for Thunderhead "to get out of their house." Out of the corner of my eye I caught a glimpse of the former chair sneaking away.

In April, I had to fire one of my full-time employees, one of the two I'd fought for in D.C. just over a year before. I'd given him a warning several months before for not completing his work. Then in April, he began spreading rumors about me, lying to board members and our biggest funders that I was not backing up our computer system, that I had not informed other staff members of their duties, that I hadn't paid our insurance for our trainings, and other false claims. I suspected that he had noticed the board's constant questioning and saw an opportunity to take my job. After I fired him, I sent an eight-page report to the board answering every one of his multitude of claims.

The weight pressing my shoulders increased, but I was strong. I'd worked in fields, on boats, I'd carried far more than these lies. I could manage as long as I kept the reports and files close, as long as I could reach them, reference them when challenged, as long as I answered the phone with confidence.

Soon after that, another one of my employees, a woman I had

hired only a few months before, began demanding that we change the name of the organization, the branding, the colors we used in the brand. She sent these demands to the board. I knew it was only renter's syndrome, that it would pass as soon as she settled in and took the time to learn about the organization. Any board of a healthy organization would have known she was out of line and sent her back to me to discuss her concerns. Not my board. The weight increased, constricting my breath.

When my husband and I picked up our completed tax forms from our accountant, she scolded me for spending nearly ten thousand dollars of my personal funds again on Thunderhead business expenses, now a yearly habit—mainly the exploratory trips, but also extra supplies. She told me this was not normal, that I should stop it.

By June 2007, not one of the board members continued any active role on program committees. The new board chair, the young man from New York City, had begun using the same phrases as the former chair, calling me naïve, cutting me off mid-sentence, telling me I had no idea what was actually going on. He was no longer that sweet young advocate I'd ridden through Manhattan with, the guy who had shown me the community garden he had fought for, who made us brie sandwiches for lunch, and had joined me on Victoria's giveaway. He had become the former chair's protégé, pressing in from the other side.

In June, I was relieved to fly to Switzerland for ECF's annual meeting and surround myself with people who reminded me of the people I'd worked with in my former life.

My bike for that trip was Lorenzo, purchased from Bern's bike station. He was a svelte city bike with rear rack, fenders, and a front light. I rode Lorenzo over the Swiss Alps with the other ECF members at the end of the meeting. On the back side, Lorenzo and I shot past the guys on fancy racing bikes on the steep, winding descent from near the peaks of the Alps to the lowest valley. Lorenzo and I traveled north on trains to visit interesting cities and my Swedish family until the larger Velo-city conference to be held in Munich.

In Groningen, Netherlands I took a room at a hotel/restaurant on the outskirts with sheep grazing next to my window. I had expected to spend five days exploring this cycling city, but rain and exhaustion kept me in the room much of the time reading *The Lucifer Effect: Understanding How Good People Turn Evil* by Philip Zimbardo. I'd bought the hardcover as soon as it was published, hoping to find explanations for the behaviors I had been encountering. Dr. Zimbardo was the professor who had conducted the Stanford Prison Experiment with eighteen young men who had answered his ad, randomly divided into roles as prisoners or guards. He discovered that evil lurked not only within his subjects, but within himself. In his analysis of the results he showed how all of them had so easily fallen into harming each other. It started with the guards dehumanizing the prisoners to the point that anything went. For this he was rewarded with traumatic consulting jobs analyzing inconceivable abuses including those at the Abu Ghraib prison in Iraq. In *The Lucifer Effect,* Dr. Zimbardo describes the danger signs, not only in others, but within ourselves.

By the time I crawled out of that damp room and traveled onward, I had found only a disturbing comfort that such abuses are common in groups. In fact, the book seemed to say that my experiences with organizations earlier in my life had been exceptions. It had done nothing to lighten my concern.

I'd looked forward to the conference in Munich, to reconnecting with my European colleagues as well as some Thunderhead members who would make the long trip. The conference did not disappoint. I laughed and discussed and rode bikes with some of my favorite people as we took part in memorable sessions. But in the backdrop, moving amidst the shadows, I could see the former chair. He was attending along with another Chicago bicycle advocate, inseparable, moving and complaining in unison. Throughout the four-day conference, their relentless whispering boomed louder than shouting.

I gave Lorenzo to a young man working at a candy shop near downtown Munich. He was stunned, just stood there after I gave him the key and walked away. After I had walked several blocks he raced up to me on Lorenzo to give me three lollipops in appreciation.

In late June, I answered my office phone to find our newest board member on the other end. He was a program director at a national community development organization who had impressed me with his coaching skills. I thought he would bring a refreshing, broader view to our myopic board. A few moments into the call I knew he had only fallen into the same hole with the rest. He demanded to know why I did not support changing the name of Thunderhead and completely rebranding it as my new employee had suggested. Standing next to my desk, I let my shoulders succumb until my elbows dug into my thighs, trying to explain the value of a name that had been in place for a decade. Then he asked me if I would support a full year-long strategic planning process conducted by outside consultants. I flashed back to that disastrous strategic planning session we'd gone through in 2003 with the other national organization that had only resulted in faulty programs and years of lost energy. That was a speck compared to the extravagant undertaking he was proposing. I knew all too well the results of such strategic planning from our member organizations. Thunderhead would be crippled during the process, costing precious funding and staff time, for only a fancy document that no one would open again. I said no. Wrong answer. He hung up without saying goodbye.

Big Red was my bike for our training in Louisville, Kentucky in July, a red Diamond Back mountain bike I bought at a pawn shop and gave to a homeless man who we invited into our room at the end to take as much leftover lunch as he liked. When I asked if he also wanted a bike, he couldn't believe his luck.

Back in my office, I froze at the ring of the phone. This time it was another board member, one who had been on the board a few years and always seemed kind, never voicing his support of the former chair's accusations. Never countering them either. Just quiet, seemingly nice. He asked if I was depressed. I'd never been asked such a question. At that moment, pacing a circle next to my desk, my heart racing and my mind at the same rate frantically flipping through possible best answers, I was anything but depressed. I knew it because I had once been horribly depressed—the months following my final crash as a bike messenger. But the last call from a board member had ended badly with the only answer I could think of. I hesitated, pressing myself down into my chair, but finally had to say it—no. He asked me specific questions, the sort a TV shrink might ask, and I forced calm answers as I tried to assure him of my sanity. When he told me how prescription drugs had saved his life, I knew he'd diagnosed me before he dialed.

The last had pegged me as defiant, blocking strategic planning. This one had pegged me as insane.

On our early July board meeting conference call I tried, but could not shift the discussions revolving around the merger. They left me in the background, only referencing me like an object, demanding short answers about the other national organization or the bike industry association they expected to fund the merger. The former chair was silent. As I strained to block him out, I realized months had passed since he had called or emailed me. He left the call early. The others were doing his work now.

In late August, as I boarded a plane to our next training in Los Angeles, my cell phone rang. It was a woman I had recently nominated for the board—clear-headed, professional, the director of one of our most effective member organizations. She could bring sensibility back to the board. She asked me about rumors she'd heard that Thunderhead was soon to disband. I froze. Would my board do this? Yes, they would. I tried to cover my shock, convince her that we were gaining momentum, no reason to disband. She warily accepted my nomination. Another one of my nominees, a program director at the smart-growth organization, had never responded. This rumor had spread to the edges of my world and pressed me into my assigned seat. Staring at my cell phone, I clung to my worn belief that the nosedive would reverse, that someone, anyone on that board would recognize the deceit and set at least a simple majority of them straight.

Her call clouded my senses as I hunted for a bike in downtown Los Angeles, influencing its name, The Cloud, a dirty-white ten-speed Murray women's-frame mountain bike, which I gave to a man with a cane and an appreciative grin. The cloud would soon lift. It had to.

8
Best,

Four days after returning from the Los Angeles training, August 31, 2007, the Friday before Labor Day weekend when you show appreciation for your employees, my office phone rang. It was the new board chair; 3:13 p.m. New York time.

"Check your email," was all he said.

On the screen an email had just appeared with the subject line: ending executive director agreement & employment. He'd only typed a few words referring to the attached letter, signing it: Best,

I begged him to explain. He told me to read the letter. I begged him to understand how much I had sacrificed for Thunderhead. He hung up.

Jim rushed in through the front door talking about tow trucks and getting another vehicle. The engine of his car had just blown as he drove up our hill. We were to drive that night to a river trip over the long weekend, our first getaway together in six years and my first river trip in at least that long. He must have seen that something was wrong. When I found the few words to tell him, he said that beat his complaint. River trip canceled.

The chair's letter, dated that day, began Dear Ms. Knaup, as if he'd never met me before. Writing on behalf of the board, he referred to the section in my employee agreement that allowed them to fire me without cause as long as they left me at my post for 180 days following termination. I was supposed to stay on the job until March 5, 2008.

It also referenced the board meeting when they had made this decision on July 26, 2007. I had no idea that meeting had taken place. For more than a month, including at our board meeting on August 8, no one had mentioned I had been fired. Business as usual. Keep working your tail off and making big plans for Thunderhead.

After a flowery paragraph expressing their "deep appreciation to you for your hard work and commitment to the Thunderhead Alliance," the letter ended with this sentence: "At this juncture, the Board of Directors desires to move in a new direction."

Like a beaten wife returning home to straighten the furniture, I wrote frenzied notes on their misconduct, at least what I knew at that point, and how I would get my job back. I kept all my upcoming meetings, even a trip to D.C. in early October, on my calendar. I answered calls and emails, assisted my staff, as if nothing had happened. But like my mother with her knife under her pillow, I jumped at any sound and scanned emails for danger.

Sleeping pills bought me a few hours of dead sleep each night before I would wake with a start, my heart pounding as if I had just answered that call on August 31st from the new board chair. Then, having discovered where I was in place and time, I'd spend the rest of those dark hours torturing through each detail and agonizing over how each of these people could have done this, could be sleeping at that very moment.

I met with lawyers in Phoenix, presenting pages of carefully typed claims. When the third one repeated that Arizona had no law protecting against wrongful termination if there was no protection in the employee agreement or bylaws, I stared him down, not letting him go and said, "I thought the law was for justice."

"Not in Arizona," he said.

I demanded to meet with the whole board, to hear directly from all of them that they supported this decision. The meeting was set for September 20th. My stack of notes grew, carefully outlining the questions I would ask before pleading for my job back. I wrote out the methods for breaking groupthink and stopping dehumanization of others as described in *The Lucifer Effect,* imagining that at least one board member would step up to be the hero, see me as a human deserving respect, then at least a simple majority would break the spell and come to my rescue. By mid-September three of my supporters had resigned from the board. A nice gesture, but my hope for breaking the spell faded with each departure.

On September 20th, I dialed the number for the conference call, my breath in rapid puffs, heart pounding. I was dialing into a group who didn't want me, entering territory where I was no longer welcome, like barging into a street gang I expected to change. As I clicked in, I went over my lines, the lines that would win me back my dream job. Thunderhead was still my life for the next day, the next month, years to come. I simply had to get through this call and show them the mistake they'd made.

Only three of the six board members on the call spoke. The former chair was at a bus stop. He hadn't even bothered to set the time aside. He only repeated his old lines, lines from the letter that Thunderhead had to move in a new direction, that Sue had to leave, not speaking to me, but the others. The other two, including the new board chair, repeated his words to me in case I hadn't heard him. They patronized me, using my name often like I was a patient.

This went on for about fifteen minutes, me pacing tight circles between the kitchen counter and table, studying the grain in our wood floor to find that traction that would snap them out of it, show their mistake. Begging them to give me my job back with only silence in response.

A switch flipped. I stopped. Sunlight flowed in. The walls breathed out. I could see the mountains in the distance. I took the phone from my ear, squeezing it as if I could squeeze them, and hung up. I thought I would float away.

9
Shattering

The days, months, years that followed that conference call flutter like confetti in my memory, many good moments, but little to pull them together. I ran and leaped from one opportunity to the next, desperately trying to surface, to fight through the emptiness they'd left me in, because I knew if I stopped I would drown in the humiliation.

In the wee hours of the morning after that final call I founded One Street. I'd skipped the sleeping pills to let my mind race through the world of possibilities that had opened that afternoon, explaining the details to one bright star at a time outside the window to beat back the dark and the drifting nightmares. International. Everything I had loved in my job at Thunderhead, which all fell into the category of serving leaders of local bicycle organizations. I'd help bicycle organizations across six continents, Antarctica too if they called. The website would be a bicycle advocacy library, open to all, not password protected like Thunderhead's had been. And no members. Every bicycle advocacy leader could call or email anytime for help. I'd finally have my chance to prove that by helping bicycle organizations avoid common dysfunctions, the entire bicycle movement would lunge forward, increasing bicycling worldwide. I decided on the name One Street, One Planet after remembering a trip with my parents when I was six. I'd asked from the backseat of our station wagon if the street we were on connected to other streets and the world was round, wasn't there only one street? They didn't answer, but they didn't need to. When daylight appeared, I told Jim, and he said, "One Street says it all." I agreed.

I saw One Street as a direct step forward, not recognizing I was plummeting off the false pedestal I had constructed since that first bicycle conference in 2000 in Philadelphia, believing this new international nonprofit would become what I had envisioned for Thunderhead.

I gathered trusted friends and colleagues from bicycle organizations around the world. Karen was one, happily back in D.C. and eager to help. A good many were in Europe, a few in Africa and down under. We formed the board and passed bylaws that would prevent anyone from tearing it apart. All of them understood the gravity of this work, not only because of what had happened to me, but from their own experiences in groups.

As the years passed, I had to accept that One Street would never cause that intense connection I had formed with the Thunderhead members in my last few years. Maybe it is the lack of membership fees, a psychological ticket to open up—they paid, so they could tell me their darkest fears. Maybe it was the energy that I brought as I fought for my job at Thunderhead. In contrast, calls and emails at One Street hardly break the surface. I help leaders of bike organizations create programs and campaigns, work through organizational development issues, but no more desperate calls for help. I could tell myself that crises aren't happening, but I know better because organizations keep vanishing.

I know that intimacy and trust from bike organizations ended at Thunderhead, too. Supportive former board members, insiders, and partners called and emailed with details. Most appalling was that the "board meeting" held on July 26 with the sole purpose of firing me had only been attended by a sub-group of board members. None of the board members who supported me had been told about it. The same month that part of the board had held that clandestine meeting, the former board chair had secured a high-paying job at one of the bike industry's largest corporations to manage their advocacy fund. Also that month, he had arranged to move

Thunderhead into the office of the national organization he wanted Thunderhead to merge with. Soon after moving into that office, they changed the name and the brand, then began the merger talks in earnest. Five years later, after funneling tragic amounts of time and resources into the merger, it failed. The organization once known as the Thunderhead Alliance spun in place regurgitating the materials I had developed with my staff. Then they transferred their remaining funds and resources over to that national organization and vanished.

After they fired me, I stayed in my home office, building a new computer, creating One Street's website, embarrassed by the space in the file cabinet at my side that had once been jammed with files about bicycle organizations, Thunderhead's members, which I'd had to pack up and send away. I didn't know I had forgotten how to live, just kept trying to do the same thing I'd been doing for five and half years, without the calls or emails. Most people I'd known through Thunderhead, at least in the United States, stopped contacting me. I was so ashamed I didn't dare reach out to them, wouldn't have dreamed of going to a conference or gathering where they might be.

Because I had lost contact with my friends from before Thunderhead, I didn't long for them, didn't even know how essential to my previous happiness they had been, how essential they would be to my recovery. I shuffled and filed, researched and posted, frantic to keep the same pace building a spectacular organization. I was a shell that had been emptied of contents that never belonged, but its residue remained. The slightest sound made me jump—the house settling, a dog bark. For years, sleep came like a battle, forcing away the sound of that new board chair's voice, "Check your email." Nightmares followed the theme of people I trusted turning into villains. I woke each morning tired, old, hollow, having to rally enthusiasm for One Street just to get up. Any hint of disrespect, even a customer in a store acting badly, sent me into a rage. I still have this, though I've learned to control it somewhat. Anything that recalled August 31, 2007 could pull the world out from under me leaving only sheer, spinning terror. Just writing this book has taken me ten years. Chapter 8 was the hardest.

I finally looked up my symptoms and found that I likely suffer from post-traumatic stress disorder (PTSD). While I am adapting to these symptoms, I can't expect to lose them. Like a veteran who saw too much, I suppose I witnessed my spirit being blown into tiny shards that day.

I see the board chair every once in a while, either at the biannual bike conference in Europe or the annual bike industry show in Las Vegas. I use him as my gauge for recovery. He even emailed me once, less than a year after that call, demanding details about bicycle organizations I'd worked with in Europe as if I was still his puppet. I corralled my panic and blew him off with one line. I could scan the crowd at a conference and find his frizzy grey hair sticking up above the others, then keep him in my peripheral vision. I thought I was getting better.

Then four years after they fired me, I was in a windowless basement meeting room in Seville, Spain with the European bike advocates wrapping up their annual meeting, all of us standing and circling into smaller groups to catch up and plan dinner. I turned from one group, trying to catch the attention of a woman who had asked me for a One Street document, my face toward the only door as I made the turn, when he burst through that door. The air between us whirled into a mortar shell exploding into my chest. I spun away, forcing a smile to my friends and colleagues as I focused on each step toward and out the door. Couldn't go to dinner with my friends. Couldn't eat. Just rode, cycling around Seville's narrow streets until exhaustion led me to my hidden hotel in the old town, then drove me up the stairs to the roof. Even now I can see each roof line, each antenna, each star I saw that night through my tears as I cursed myself for being so weak. Since then, each sighting has diminished, now just a curiosity to be avoided.

While sightings of the board chair and others from that time drag me back to that emptiness, my friends have filled me back up. Wallace Stegner uses a metaphor in his novels that people who are important to us become our mirrors. When we are near them, we can see our true selves. My friends came back to me, or maybe they'd never left, just left me alone during that time. With them, I rebuilt myself.

My friend Johanna, only ten minutes away, had patiently waited nearly six years until I wasn't "so busy," listened intently to my horror story, then brought me a remedy. A fundraiser for PAT was coming up and she wondered if we could make something for the auction. I had recommended Gayle as the auctioneer and they hired her.

Johanna and I met at my old bike shop on a tree-shaded dirt back street, which had become my personal workshop after moving the bike shop to the main road in its sixth year. Entering the shop through the double doors, I tasted a hint of the pride I'd known as the owner-operator of Ironclad Bicycles in its early days.

The large windows across the back wall light the open room with mottled sun through the entwined trees along the creek out back. Below the center window sits my long workbench with sloping tool board, vice, and wheel-truing stand, my bike repair stand a few steps from it. To either side of the bench sit several cabinets and cubbies of bike parts. To the left, along the far wall, I have lined up and hung on the wall the best of my antique-bike collection, which I started after my last crash as a bike messenger. If I couldn't ride those old bikes as a messenger anymore, at least I could collect them.

Space was a bit of an issue back when I had to fit a whole bike shop in there. Plus, back then, I supplemented the bike sales and repair income with welding jobs that often accounted for half of the year's income. My welding machine and table sit in the middle of the workshop surrounded with more tool boxes, my drill press, and the massive anvil Jim gave me one year for Christmas. So all the bikes for sale went outside each day to allow me room to work. When I moved the bike shop a few blocks away onto the main road, the workshop became my own tinkering place, a refuge I needed all the more in those desperate days. Johanna's excuse to go play there came just in time.

Though Johanna is twenty years my senior, our friendship

seems like one started in elementary school between life-long buds. She's an artist and community activist, proud of the projects she's organized for her neighborhood, tall and animated, preferring to act out her points rather than waste time on words. Sometimes she gets too obsessed over the latest news, but who am I to scold her about obsession?

We pulled old, broken bikes and scrap metal from the back shed and around the outside of the workshop, scattering them around the concrete driveway. Passersby must have wondered what these two women were doing pondering all that metal junk. We placed and bundled bits that seemed to need each other, then pieced them together into the weirdest sculptures with wheels and bike frames stacked and twisted. I did the welding, dragging the results back out to the driveway for her approval, delivered in the form of hysterical laughter. Somewhere along the way, we named ourselves Grunt Design (I'm the Grunt, she's Design), so I signed them with my welding torch G.D. She finished them off with bright pastel paints.

Gayle came into town with her welcome buoyant spirit, uplifting me all the more, and sold those four Grunt Design sculptures for hundreds of dollars each at the PAT auction. At least one of those first sculptures is still around, decorating a hip motel near downtown. We try to do at least one project each year now. Johanna reintroduced me to the part of me who values art, looking around corners of things, imagining them rearranged, held in a new light, not stuck in dark shadows.

In Knut, my Swedish brother, I rediscovered the part of me who takes the world head on. When a tractor wheel falls off and there's no spare part or store open, Knut makes that part out of scrap metal. When a crop is frozen or flooded, he turns his energy to another. Five and half years had fallen out of my life. Time to move on.

From Heidi, my Swedish sister, I relearned how to appreciate myself, to trust each moment. One afternoon, sitting in her kitchen, lifting my eyes from the blond-wood floor so common in Swedish homes, to glance past fresh flowers out the white-gloss-trimmed window across the dirt farm road to Knut's house, I told her my tale of woe. She listened, her deep blue eyes following my pain, then gave me a beer, cracking her own and raising it with an emphatic "Skål!"

My other family, my blood family, played their own strange role in my recovery. My mother had been diagnosed with or identified as likely having or whatever the terminology is for Alzheimer's disease. She was living here in Prescott, in the house next to my workshop, which I'd previously rented out. When my Uncle Den had died in the late '90s, my cousins had kicked her out of the house he'd bought for her in Mill Valley, California, her hometown where she and her father had grown up, where she had tried to raise me and my brother.

The disease got so frightening to her that she ran off every caregiver Prescott had to offer, sure they were going to attack her. She was too frail and confused to move into our small house with our big dogs and steep stairs. When all the options were exhausted, I worked with the county health providers to find her a room at a supportive home in Sedona that specializes in the disease. Guilt twisted my gut the evening I had to leave her there. It was New Year's Eve. We'd waited in the hall for nearly an hour. She commented about the other patients walking by, how much healthier she was. I joked with her that she would teach them a thing or two about healthy living. When the nurse finally came to get her, I began to walk away then turned, realizing I'd better remind her that I would return to visit soon.

"See you next year, Mom," I said.

"Don't you say that to your mother!" a man who had been sitting several chairs from us said.

I realized my mistake and thanked him. "Mom," I said, "I mean I'll see you next week, okay?"

Her blank stare broke into a smile. "I'll see you soon, Sweety."

Within a few months there she fell in love with another patient named George. When I'd visit, I'd find them sitting close together in a corner of the sunny common room, her telling stories about her childhood in Mill Valley, him soaking them up. I'd bring along my Great Dane-mix, Chloe, who always sparked her story about her Saint Bernard who had pulled her from the surf when she was a toddler.

After a year of bliss, George's wife moved him back home and my mom began slipping away. On my return from a trip to Europe, a nurse called, frantic that I should come.

I arrived on her last day here. Could tell the moment I walked in her room. She had shriveled down to a skeleton, her only signs of life were the puffs of air she forced out of her pursed lips. I sat on her bed holding her hand, telling her how much I loved her. She whimpered in response. After a long time like that, I got up, not knowing what to do. I didn't want to sleep there that night, no place for me anyway. I went out into the hall, cornered a nurse and asked her. She said I should do whatever felt right.

I sat down in the middle of a line of chairs along the hall wall, dumbfounded, bewildered. I'd never been in charge of anyone's death before. How can you be in charge of someone else's last hurrah? This was her moment and I felt like an intruder. Fortunately, a kind, middle-aged man sat down next to me. After introducing himself he began informing me in great detail about how the nurses kept track of them through the electrical wall outlets. There was an outlet right across the hall from us, so he had a prime example to show me. I delved in, asking for clarification on the electrical circuitry and scanners that sent beacons from the outlets to read their wristbands until I was an expert on this nurse-espionage device. By the time he left, I was ready. I went back in, sat down, held her hand, and told her goodbye. Told her it was okay to go. That she'd been a great mom, protector, role model, and friend. She could move on if she liked. She died in the first few hours of the next morning.

I was in the middle of arranging her cremation and planning her memorial in Mill Valley when a sheriff from Marin County called. My brother, Steve, had committed suicide. I hadn't seen him since I was twenty after the restraining order had sent him out into the world. We'd heard from him only a few times in those twenty-six years. He knew nothing about our mother's dementia or that she had died. Perhaps ten years had passed since they'd spoken over the phone. I knew he'd been a limousine chauffeur, a channel for his spiritual leader, and had serviced computers. He'd also been in love with a man who had died. In Steve's suicide note he said he was going to see him.

My first thought when I heard this news was that Steve finally got his wish. Then I asked what day he had died. It was the very same day my mother had died. I don't know how that could have happened. I don't know if there is some sort of connection between blood relatives, perhaps the sorrow they shared. He was her first baby, so she could never accept it when he tried to harm her. And she was his mom.

My husband, Jim, was the friend who helped me through those strange days. His family is close. They support each other and crowd around the phone to talk with us on major holidays. I don't expect him to understand the peculiar trio that was my mother, brother, and me. Jim was just there, even took me out in his skiff on a Prescott lake that winds between mottled granite outcroppings and groves of shimmering cottonwood trees, feeding me beers as I sat in the bow shaking my head saying, "I'll be darned, I'll be darned," over and over, oddly relieved. Relieved my mother hadn't known. Relieved Steve had gotten his wish. Relieved that the threat of Steve, that maybe he would show up in Prescott, was gone.

Five years after Thunderhead, I was rushing into the grocery store when I nearly slammed into my dear tennis buddy Dana. He's just taller than me, not quite six feet, fit, almost regal in his stature with his white hair and cropped beard. But the glint in his eye reveals his kind heart, sprinkled just right with his twisted sense of humor that made us friends from the start. His invitation to join an afternoon tennis group at his neighborhood tennis courts in the cool breezes and soft shadows of the pine forest south of town led to new friends and the return of the joy of tennis.

I found time at Christmas to reach out to lost friends—each of their cards in return a needed spark of joy. One in particular sent me over the moon. He didn't bother with a card, just picked up the phone and called me on Christmas day. I knew his voice immediately, that and the fact that all he said was, "Cream Cheese!" It was my precious friend Pig, my second dispatcher as a San Francisco bike messenger in the '80s.

The first time we met, I hated him because he wasn't Mad Dog. After my first winter riding, I'd left for about a year—summers river guiding, hitchhiking in the fall, two semesters at Prescott College. Sparkies had moved from that cave of a garage on Clementina alley to a brighter, more spacious garage and office on Third Street. I charged in through the open garage door that morning, ready to take my first delivery instructions from Mad Dog in the dispatcher booth to the right of the door. But all I saw in there was this small, wiry guy with sharp brown eyes and nineteen earrings dangling from his ears. I glared at him and he glared back. I asked where Mad Dog was and he said, "Gone."

"Who are you?"

"Call me Pig. Who are you?"

"Sue. Number's 25."

"Sorry, 25's taken. You're number 31 now."

I flung my sweater at him since the dispatch booth seemed like the only place to store it for the day. He slapped my first tag of the day onto the shelf and turned to the next messenger.

I had to admit as I followed his routes that he had a knack, though I didn't admit it easily. He'd lay out a line like Market to Chinatown to Market and I'd talk back like who was he kidding. He didn't waste words.

"Cream Cheese," took me a moment to get the association to my name (Mothers of Invention), "Stockton Tunnel."

Right. I'd be at the tunnel in Chinatown and could shoot through right to the door of that last pick-up.

I rode in that night still suspicious of the guy. I wrote out my tags with the rest of the messengers at the picnic tables near the back then took them to his booth, slapping them down on the shelf and demanding my sweater. He turned, took it off a table, and handed it to me. I was speechless. He'd folded it.

That melted my ice and from then on we hit it off. He invited me and a few other messengers to dinner at his and his boyfriend's house. They had two big mutts, both rescues, and I had my Meshab, a Black Lab/German Shepherd mix I'd adopted from the Marin Humane Society when I worked there. Pig and I started taking the dogs to Golden Gate Park or the beach on the weekends. Over the years, he became so essential to me that when I came back to San Francisco from my seven-month-long hitching trip around the world to find that he had moved to Harrisburg, Pennsylvania, I was devastated. Our weekends walking and talking and playing with dogs had to be replaced with the phone.

Hearing his voice in that broken time shot me back to our days in San Francisco when I was courageous and surfing the world. Nothing and no one could harm me back then. I played with death all day and felt life all the more. Pig reminded me that I could live free and happy. Had before and so could again.

Another group of friends reflected my broken side, the side that never should have tolerated abuse. My first tries at this book came from my anger, all bitter resentment. I thought it was fine, ready for readers to help me rearrange the sentences a bit. I joined a writers' critique group with friends I knew from the local writers association, some before Thunderhead. They did not hold back in their critiques—red slashes with words like "poisoned" and "rampant paranoia." After a drastic reality check, I discovered that I had left myself out entirely, creating a book with no main character, only a list of abuses, tempered with Bike Hunts. I set it aside.

Then my friend Jeffe reentered my life with an email. We had been river guides together on the Stanislaus River in California starting in 1979 when I was fifteen and he was twenty-five. He was the permit holder for our forty-five-day Grand Canyon river trip that same year and helped me get established as a guide in Utah. Attached to his email was a rough draft of his memoir from that time when he was fighting through a cancer diagnosis that came during another adventure we were on with a few other river guides. The trip was supposed to be six weeks from Wyoming to Arizona on the Yampa, Green, and Colorado rivers. We spent it instead in hospitals as they sliced away parts of him then ripped him open from sternum to crotch to scrape the cancer away.

More than thirty years later I found myself reliving that story on my computer screen, then learning all the parts I'd missed. My story, forgotten and left entirely out of my own memoir, became richer from reading his. His daring spirit, temporarily crushed by the disease, came back to me along with the times he had sparked my own.

At Lava Falls, the biggest drop in Grand Canyon, not long after his recovery from surgery, we were scouting the rapid from a flat-topped lava boulder with a group of new guides. From the scout you can see the whole expanse of plummeting white foam cradled by the towering maroon, gold, and grey cliffs of the canyon. As we studied the treacherous right run of the rapid, Jeffe turned to me and said, "You lead 'em in." I argued that I was far younger than any of them, but he wouldn't back down, said I was the most experienced and had to do it. He was rowing sweep. I'll never forget that first sight from my boat of Lava's edge without any boat ahead, the river sliding past the shear lava cliffs, no more pullouts, Lava's famous silence before the drop, feeling each grain of my wooden oar handles, knowing the trainees would follow me in. Jeffe knew I could do it even before I did.

Reading his memoir so many years later reunited me with my former, daring, river-guide self. I had a thought. Would he, could he read mine once I rewrote it? He would indeed. We'd started a new adventure together.

I began filling this book, refilling myself, with the person I had been before Thunderhead. As I came back to life through words and stories, the Thunderhead people diminished and my bitterness eased. Without these friends during my time at Thunderhead, I had mutated, no longer able to see my own reflection—and that mutant remained even after that sub-group of board members had discarded me. How utterly lonely and empty it had been. These old friends enabled me to see myself again, then try myself on like a forgotten favorite shirt. Once back on, the memories of my former self swirled back and became the present, became who I am. With my friends I can appreciate myself again, in action, play off them as if in a dance with myself. I know now that these friends, these mirrors, are critical because without them I lost everything.

I fought to forgive myself for tossing five and a half of my most impassioned years to Thunderhead. Sure, I discovered how to help bicycle organization leaders. But I made that discovery in the first year. Had I recognized the abuse as I had as a child, I could have saved at least four of those years with a graceful resignation and founded One Street on a high note with more realistic expectations.

I leapt at any hint of traction for One Street. I was invited to Prague to teach bicycle advocates how to plan campaigns, but they allowed me only an afternoon and none of the attendees were prepared. Nothing came of it.

I answered a call to Budapest, where bicycle advocates said they were ready to start their own Social Bike Business program. After weeks of meetings in two trips over two years, nothing came of it.

I knew these and other organizations I was working with around the world were suffering from the same damaging group behaviors I'd discovered at Thunderhead, but I no longer had the intimate connection I needed to guide them back on track. I eventually captured the warning signs and my guidance in my book, *Cures for Ailing Organizations.* If they were no longer calling with these deep troubles at least there would be a chance they could find help in my book.

Prescott has delivered its share of dysfunction reminders. While I was serving as president of a local nonprofit, the executive director accused me of behavior I'd been victim to at Thunderhead. I stepped down. I was invited by a close friend to serve on another board she chaired. My last moments on that board are as clear as this moment.

I'm standing at the head of the polished-wood table that takes up most of the private room adjacent to a downtown restaurant. I've taped blank sheets of paper on the wall as I did each year for Thunderhead's annual meeting. My friend couldn't make this meeting, so she asked me to run it, to wrap up our discussion on the organization's mission statement. The other board members are seated around the table, talking in small groups, ignoring me. The terror builds as I recognize their behavior, see flashes of the Thunderhead board.

But Pig died this morning. My precious friend checked into the hospital a few weeks ago feeling like he had the flu and came out a corpse—cancer of the liver. I'll never see him again. I'm still shaking from the news. Or is it the behavior of these board members? Any other day I'd be strong, could block the flashbacks. The room tightens, their chatter presses my ears. There's a glass door behind me leading to the street. I make a few more feeble attempts, then roll up the papers, take my pens, and step out that door.

Years after that awful board meeting, those individuals greet me like a friend. I see them in that meeting no matter where we meet and ponder as they chitchat how they could have treated me so disrespectfully. Board and staff members I worked with at Thunderhead do the same when I am unfortunate enough to encounter them at the bike industry trade show or the European conference, but I don't engage their chitchat.

Prescott also offered a necessary step toward recovery, though my lingering bitterness kept me from seeing it right away. Only months after I was fired, a professor at Prescott College asked for my help with a semester-long bicycle course he wanted to teach. I imagined it becoming a long-term course there, taught by any teacher with a love for bikes. So we captured every step to make it a turnkey course. After two springs of co-teaching it with him, he handed it off to me. I gave my next three springs to that course, improving it each year.

Three days a week, I took my students through bicycle facility design, showed them how to teach people how to ride, taught them campaign planning, and took them to City Hall and the Prescott engineering department to request improvements for bicycling as they should in any city. Some joined me at two European bike conferences. Each student received a carrying case of the tools they'd need to fix most bikes and a thick repair manual, which they used to strip down a used bike to rebuild and give away at the end of the class, passing on the Bike Hunt.

Fridays were reserved for this mechanic training. On the first Friday I'd line up the bikes I'd gathered in the prior months through donations or at thrift stores. They had to be adult sized, quality (no BSOs), and have external gears so the students could learn derailleur adjustments. Those hunts for bikes around town gave me a needed taste of the Bike Hunt and an excuse to do a bit of work on them at my workshop to ensure they had all their parts. I'd introduce each bike to the half circle of students including their best qualities and possible repair headaches. Once each student had chosen their bike and had their tools and manual ready, I'd go over the basics of disassembly and then let them rip.

Sitting cross-legged on the ground between campus buildings, surrounded by parts and wheels, the bike frames in their laps, sometimes paired or grouped to share their puzzlement, my students eased into bicycle infatuation. Some metal tubes, a ring of metal or rubber, some ball bearings, and random parts are nothing but scattered objects. But if you hold this set of tubes up just right, add grease to these particular ball bearings before sliding them into place on this other set of tubes, you can fit one into the other so it turns just right and becomes the front fork assembly where one wheel will attach, then the other wheel to the back, and the seat and handlebar and chain and pedals and tires and brakes all fall into place to become this magical machine that enables people to traverse cities and scale mountains.

Assembled bikes did not complete their course, though. In order to get credit, my students had to find an appropriate recipient for their bike—not someone who already had a bike or wanted one to sell. Someone whose life would be improved by a bike. I learned to start them on this recipient hunt early in the course because none of them were used to this sort of thing. Each week I'd ask if they'd found a bike recipient. Sometimes I had to help. If recipients wanted, they could join the students to finish their bikes. Watching my shy, nervous students push their bikes into waiting hands, I saw the Bike Hunt disperse into the world.

The course consumed those springs with class preparations, correcting papers, guiding each student through their particular fears, and the students just left. That last day I'd show them what they'd accomplished and encourage them to run with it, to make the world better with bicycles. But they'd just walk away, leaving me to fill out their evaluations like incident reports. When I told the school I needed to pass the course on to a new teacher, they dropped it.

Then, over time, I was treated to chance encounters with some of my students. An email describing how one had built his own bike and trailer and was organizing his neighborhood to shop by bike. Walking into a bike shop in San Francisco looking for a used bike to find one of my former students greeting me as their manager. Reports from one of my most talented students helping to grow a wildly successful bike program for inner-city kids in Philadelphia, thanking me for the bike course that led her to her new career. Spending five spring semesters buried in class prep and papers seemed like a good price to pay for all of that.

My bitterness also clouded the success of another unexpected opportunity. An email arrived from a founding leader of a budding organization in rural southwestern Uganda. They envisioned a nonprofit that would empower women by teaching them career skills. They would raise money by renting bicycles to the tourists who traveled to their village to visit the Impenetrable Forest, a dense primeval forest that had survived the ice age with plants and animals found nowhere else on Earth, including the last mountain gorillas. When I asked if they planned to teach the women bicycle mechanic skills and how to start their own bike shops, he said of course. That's when he got me.

That Ugandan odyssey stretched over four years including two trips there. I fell in love with the place, the rain forest like a hundred-foot-thick carpet draping sheer mountains surrounding the village, the villagers who were so eager to learn and help, the women who attended my classes—some of my best students. The first trip required lots of fundraising to pay for tools and more bikes for their rental fleet. We used those bikes to teach basic repair and riding skills to hundreds of local women.

The second trip, two years later, was better planned. My fundraising paid for the building of the organization's new bicycle workshop. On that trip, I spent my first week helping them organize the bikes, the workshop, and the women who would take part. Then I taught a week-long course in advanced bicycle mechanics to eight eager women who planned to open their own bike shops in their villages. Some walked for miles each morning to attend this high-level tech training, each student stripping a rental bike to the frame to rebuild it. They learned bearing adjustments, wheel truing, and repair options for remote areas. Each day also included business training—working with customers, diagnosing and taking in repairs, even managing staff. When they graduated, they received an official certificate and their own bicycle.

But each day started with a knot in my stomach. As I ate my breakfast at a gorilla conservation camp across the dirt road from the workshop with a few other volunteers who were working in the area, I went over the warning signs. The organization leaders had been rude to me from the start of the trip and didn't attend any of my classes. These women were their clients and, had the leaders attended, they could have learned the mechanic skills to teach more women. As the days progressed, I realized they'd given up on bikes. Another donor had given them money to buy sewing machines and fabric. They were spending their days teaching other women how to sew items that the organization would then sell to tourists—iPad covers, cellphone pouches, tablecloths. This was no simple confusion over their mission. They had discarded it entirely in order to chase a new funding source. The paint on their brand new bicycle workshop hadn't even dried, but I knew that after I left it would become storage, the tools I'd brought abandoned. I swallowed my sorrow for the rest of the trip to focus my attention on my eight students as they learned their new skills.

I'm afraid I stumbled while I was there, missing the next step to recovery right in front of me: gratitude for the opportunity to help these eight extraordinary women onto their own next steps in life. Now I know that the only way I have ever and will ever change the world is through direct interaction with people who value what I have to offer. My desperate need for Bike Hunts while I was at Thunderhead demonstrates how far I had strayed from this fundamental truth.

I offered campaign trainings at the European gatherings, but they were usually scheduled for the end of the day, my time whittled down as other sessions ran over. What I knew took three days to teach properly had to be jammed into ridiculously short segments. Once, my scheduled two hours was cut to fifteen minutes. I stood, defined what a campaign was, sent my stack of handouts around the room, and sat back down, fighting my urge to scream at the endless procession of disappointments.

Recently, during a coffee break at the European bicycle conference in Nantes, France, a bike advocate from Ukraine who I've seen at the gatherings for many years, came up to me to tell me they were still using my campaign planning handout. Later that year, he asked me to train him and his colleague to teach bicycle campaign trainings as part of a project to reunite their country through bicycles. They conducted three successful trainings, engaging local advocates in twelve bicycle and sustainable transportation campaigns in the east near the frontline—pedestrian zones, access for disabled people on streets and public transit, bikeways on main roads through their cities. I then spent nearly two weeks there working with them in groups and intimate meetings, to finalize their campaign plans. A few months later my colleague, the advocate who'd approached me in France, sent a report showing that not only was every campaign succeeding, but many had exceeded their expectations. Not bad for a fifteen-minute talk.

I'm gently piecing myself back together, like the next Grunt Design project. With each success at One Street, I carefully allow the activist back in. A sprint through traffic transforms my grips back to my messenger bike and for that moment I'm racing the clock to the next delivery. A whiff of diesel exhaust hints at the hot, hard asphalt road edge and the rumble of it stretching away to new discoveries.

For my fiftieth birthday, I started on my bucket list with a week at a tennis camp near Tampa, Florida where champions hone their games. I stayed with an Airbnb host nearby and found a bike on my first day after hours of hunting along endless speedways that connected scattered strip-mall developments across long swaths of swampland. When I finally approached downtown Tampa I found a pedestrian to ask and he sent me to a pawn shop where I found Chrystal—a sleek, white, women's-frame bike, the sort you see in Amsterdam. I rode her each morning along a typical, glaring speedway before that refreshing dip down the camp road through the thick tree canopy and into the clearing where the first spread of twenty-five tennis courts would appear.

On my birthday, I skipped the tennis to ride out to a swamp preserve with bike paths wending through the droopy, moss-covered trees and dark bogs. I raced a storm back, its wind pushing me faster than the cars. When the wall of rain hit me, I took shelter at a mini mart and hitched a ride the rest of the way with three construction workers in a muddy pickup.

When the week of tennis camp wrapped up, I gave Chrystal to my host, who planned to give her to his girlfriend so they could ride together.

The next summer, I picked off two more bucket-list items: attending the Wimbledon tennis championship and cycling around the Yorkshire Moors in England—steep rounded mountains that had been carved by glaciers, their crags and grassy cliffs like no other place on Earth.

My arrival in Yorkshire provided an unexpected chance to engage my withered hitchhiking skills. Buses were parked outside the Malton train station, so at first I figured I'd find one heading my way. I'd booked a room at a farmhouse at the top of a remote moor. This was England, not the United States. Buses go everywhere. Sure enough there was a bus that would have taken me to within about five miles of my farmhouse, but it wouldn't leave for another two hours. The bus station manager seemed genuinely sorry for stranding me, even resorting to calling a few bus drivers who were getting off work to see if they were going my way. No luck.

Hitchhiking didn't even occur to me until I was out the door pondering my backpack and where to sit wasting those excruciating two hours when I could have been in the moors. My thumb twitched and a savvy grin spread across my face. I stepped back into the station and asked the manager to draw me a road map to my moor.

Walking out of Malton to the north road along the left, not right, side of the road, a giddiness grew as I anticipated turning around and thrusting out my thumb. Each car that passed was a missed ride, but I knew I had to find a straight section if they were going to stop. I finally found it, a long section between cross streets across from a cricket ground. A tall hedge lined my side of the sidewalk. On the back side, a gardener was trimming the hedge. When he got to me, small chunks of hedge rained down. I considered walking on, but decided to give the spot a chance. Plus, I'd never spent any time watching cricket. The guys in white across the road were behaving strangely with awkward bats and a tiny ball.

I held my thumb out, proud and confident in my all-but-forgotten skill. Many cars passed, but I knew I only needed one. Before half an hour was up a dark-blue compact eased to a stop next to me and I opened the door to learn the driver was going a short way in my direction. He was visiting his former home from his current home in Barbados, happy to get me closer to my destination. From his pull-off in open, flat farmland, I caught a ride with a construction worker to Pickering, the closest full-sized town to my moor. I had to walk a few miles to get past the local traffic, past the small shops and oily stench of fish and chips, swinging around to thrust out my thumb at each car that passed. Before I reached the other side of Pickering, Sammie pulled over in a small SUV, rolled down the window and laughed when I told her where I was heading. She lived at a farm on the same moor. After taking me to her home to meet her kids and have a cup of tea, she dropped me off right at my farmhouse. My hosts even had a bike for me to ride—a women's-frame, fifteen-speed mountain bike—no need for a Bike Hunt.

I spent ten extraordinary days living and bicycling on the moors through wafts of coal fires, manure, and moist stone walls that reminded me of so many hitchhiking trips through the U.K. in my youth, bahing back at sheep, drawn into village pubs by the laughter. Those days pedaling were contrasted with two more chances to hitchhike when my chosen destinations were farther than I could reach by bike in one day.

Standing at a busy junction in Pickering holding my sign to Whitby, I felt my long ago pride in the freedom to go wherever and whenever I chose. No bus schedules, though I could have taken a bus that time. On the way back, I caught a ride with Sammie's husband who owned a clothing store in Whitby and had offered a ride on his commute home.

All I'd needed was to revive the skills I'd learned as a teenager—where to stand, how to present myself, and the courage to trust the people passing in their isolated metal boxes.

10
This

Many of the people who picked me up when I was hitchhiking in my youth told me sad stories. That's saying a lot because I hitchhiked for months every fall for nine years and took random trips after that. Each leg of a journey could have a dozen rides. That's a lot of sad people.

Some regretted a particular turn in their lives, resenting the forces from society that seemingly caused them to take that turn, no choice. A common theme was going to university to get a job they'd never wanted. These rides often drove fancy cars well above the speed limit as if to prove that forfeiting their life had been worth it, even as their stories proved otherwise. But the drivers of cheaper, beat-up cars weren't immune. They often told me about demanding parents, sadistic spouses, and too many kids, a job they hated but had to keep just to feed their family. Too many of these stories started with grand ambitions only to end in disappointment.

As a hitchhiker, I found that magic key that opened them up to me, similar to what I achieved at Thunderhead when the leaders of member organizations began calling with their horror stories. I suppose that as a hitchhiker, I was so anonymous I hardly existed in their world. They could reveal their darkest regret, knowing that as soon as I got out of their car I would vanish along with their secret.

Every ride who told me such a tale included a warning to me—

to enjoy life while I was young, before the inevitable grabbed hold of me and ended my freedom. They'd say they wished they could drop everything and hit the road as I was doing. I'd ask why they didn't and never got an answer better than, "I can't."

Oddly, many of these rides, after issuing their firm warning to stay free and on the road as long as I possibly could, would ask me what I wanted to do when I "grew up." They would morph into the societal force that they had a moment before despised. Rather than call them on their hypocrisy, I came up with an answer that seemed to capture what I wanted to do with my life: "This."

That single word would often end the discussion, which was my main goal. But as the years of road travel progressed, I found a deeper meaning in that word, especially because some rides grilled me further.

"This," they'd say. "You mean you want to just hitchhike around for the rest of your life?"

"No," I'd say. "I mean what I'm doing right now. I'm talking with you, responding to your questions."

That usually got their attention. "You can't stay with me."

"No, you don't get my meaning. I am responding to what the world has presented to me at this moment. This, at this moment, happens to be talking with you. When you let me out, I'll get another ride and that will present a different 'this.' Does that make sense?"

"So you're just going to go along and respond to whatever happens?"

"Yeah," I'd say with an approving smile. "Now you've got it."

That answer never failed to send them into a glazed-eye silence as they tried to imagine what their lives would have been had they simply done "this" before getting stuck in their rut. My little mind-game turned out to be two-way, though, because as they sat there pondering, I was left to do the same, the two of us gazing onto the rushing highway trying to capture snapshots of this in the past, present, and future.

Back then I didn't have to ponder my future long because I believed in this. Every once in a while, though, my belief got a bit rattled—especially when I got stuck. Something about moving contented me, but if I had to stand in one place for more than a few hours a grumbling frustration would dig its way in. Amarillo, Texas and Barstow, California were the two suckholes that never failed to latch me in place. In Amarillo, it was a particular overpass on the west side of the city along Interstate 40 just too far to walk into town. Truck drivers going into the city had to take an off-ramp right before that overpass. Sometimes heading west when a trucker would tell me he was stopping in Amarillo, the thought of that dreaded overpass would tempt me to turn down the ride. But I never did, just succumbed to that long wait kicking at the road debris that accumulated there, just like me.

But Barstow takes the record for my longest wait. I'd been dropped off there the evening before and slept next to the dry wash that ties together the windswept bones of the town. I walked in dread to the junction I knew all too well—a T-intersection where the highway west splits from the main drag south. I got there at sunrise. By mid-afternoon I was ready to scream. That's about when Charlie sauntered up to me. He was a tall, skinny elderly man in dusty black work pants, black button-down shirt, and twisted cowboy hat, like an old west gun fighter who'd had more than his share of luck.

"Standin' here long?" he asked.

"Since the beginning of time."

"No really, when'd you start?"

"Sunrise."

"Bah," he spat through his laugh, "That ain't nothin'. I've been hitching since I was younger than you and learned to settle in for days sometimes. S'pose it's easier for gals, though. You just have to stay in the moment. This moment, the moment we're in is all that matters. Then you won't get frustrated."

We introduced ourselves and I eased into his calm as he continued his lecture to go light on my circumstances, appreciate the sights around me. I nearly sputtered back when he waved his hand around the desolate sand, parched wood, and peeling paint that was Barstow, admonishing me to understand its beauty.

"You look like you need something to eat," Charlie said after a good while. "Did you know that you are just steps away from the best chili in this here United States?"

He urged me to follow him, though I couldn't help peering back at the cars passing, wondering if I was missing my one and only ride that day. I followed him for several blocks west along the highway before we cut right onto a side street and into the screened back door of what seemed to be a house with its white peeling paint and clothesline in the yard. But it turned out to be a small local restaurant. We'd entered the kitchen, but I could see the tables filled with customers through the open door leading to the front.

"Charlie, nice to see you, dear," said the rugged middle-aged woman, clearly the proprietress.

Charlie introduced us and asked her to give me one of the bowls of chili she'd promised him each day he stayed in Barstow. She sat me down in the kitchen and brought me an enormous bowl of dark-red chili thick with ground beef and beans. After my first bite I told Charlie he wasn't lying about it being the best chili in the country. The proprietress beamed.

"You take your time with that chili, enjoy it," Charlie said, "When you're done, you'll be all straightened out and you'll get your ride." Then he left.

Charlie was right. About fifteen minutes after I stepped back onto that highway, I caught a ride going all the way into Bakersfield. After that, whenever I got stuck for most of a day, in Barstow or wherever, I'd remember Charlie, then let the moment be. Once I was back on track, someone would pull over and set me in motion once again. Charlie's lecture that day was the seed that became my belief in this.

This can be a dangerous way to live if you veer off course. Many of my rides were already doing this, stuck in lives they never wanted.

But I was happy and content when I was hitchhiking, so I could present this as my grand ambition. I actually followed this right up until my time at Thunderhead, each step in my life responding to the last. I escaped my brother by taking the job at the humane society, which led to the jobs at the wildlife center and lobbying for animal rights, which led me to the Stanislaus and my career as a river guide, which led me to hitchhiking, which led me to Sweden and my first true home and family. River guiding also led me to my job as a bike messenger. When I was hit by the Cadillac, my bike messenger career ended, but my new one as a bike shop owner followed because of it. As a bike shop owner I realized Prescott needed street improvements if more people were going to choose bicycling, so I founded Prescott Alternative Transportation (PAT) by tapping my past experience with nonprofits. Each step was a close steppingstone away from the last. This, intentionally or not, kept me on a path of contentment and happiness.

I don't know when I first strayed from this. It wasn't sudden. My ambition to change the world only started at PAT, a simple shift from contentment to discontentment. All my activism before that was merely what I did and expected to do well. Something derailed in me while I was at PAT that caused my discontentment. I'd started the organization to improve Prescott's streets and reconnect the town for bicyclists and pedestrians. Each success made me want more. I watched the bike lanes being striped and wanted every high-speed road to have them. I worked alongside dozens of volunteers as we built the Prescott Greenways Trail and wanted to keep going along every creek until all the creek-side neighborhoods connected to downtown. When the highway interchange at the entry to Prescott was rebuilt to include our pathway design I wanted every highway interchange in the country to have one, connected to bikeway networks everywhere. By the time Thunderhead finally accepted PAT as a member and I attended the Philadelphia conference, I had already given myself over to that ambition.

At Thunderhead, I learned firsthand the danger of ambition that my hitchhiking rides had warned me about. But my ambition was only one of the volatile ingredients. That they fired me is not the concern. It's clear I never should have been in that job. In fact, they could have let me go in a respectful and caring way—discussed their desired changes with me, found I didn't agree, and worked with me on the transition.

What concerns me, what has driven me to write this book, is something far more disturbing that took hold of that group and caused them to discard me like a broken piece of office furniture. I knew all but the board chair to be good and kind people. Even the board chair, stripped of his need to manipulate, could have been a good person. But in that group they became monsters. What I experienced at Thunderhead was a miniature of some of the most disturbing events in human history.

When I read *The Lucifer Effect* in my last year there, I read it to decipher the behaviors I was responding to as leaders of our member organizations called me for help. I didn't want to see that I was engulfed by the very same behaviors, including my own. In the book, Dr. Zimbardo describes his Stanford Prison Experiment, how the eighteen young men—nine randomly assigned with the flip of a coin to be guards, the other nine to be prisoners—changed within hours of entering the makeshift prison. The "prisoners" were stripped of everything that made them an individual and given only a dress-like sack to wear. They could no longer use their names, only their assigned numbers. Dehumanized. The "guards" were given uniforms and superior authority over the prisoners and told by Dr. Zimbardo to keep them in line.

The prisoners cowered to the guards. Some tried to appease them in order to gain rewards like food or bathroom privileges. Others went berserk, screaming, complaining, and crying against the abuse. When the guards accused them of being menaces to society, they actually apologized, even though they'd done nothing wrong. A few made a feeble attempt at escape, but were easily caught and tortured. None of the prisoners stood up to proclaim the experiment unjust and simply walk out of the unlocked basement. They had forgotten it was only an experiment.

The guards either became sadistic abusers or fell in line with those who were—forcing the prisoners to do obscene performances, stripping them, shutting them in closets, denying them basic necessities. After the experiment was over, Dr. Zimbardo asked one of the most brutal guards why he had done such horrible things to the prisoners. He replied, "Nobody stopped me." So he had kept going to see how much he could get away with.

The experiment was supposed to last two weeks. By day six the guards had become so violent and abusive toward the prisoners, Dr. Zimbardo had to stop the experiment. What disturbed him most is that he could have continued the experiment in the name of science, his ambition, except for the chance visit by his girlfriend on the sixth day. Her outrage over what she saw was the only thing that snapped him out of it.

In his book, Dr. Zimbardo describes the intricate system he unwittingly set in place that enabled the servitude and viciousness to take place. In his later work consulting in the aftermath of similar disgraces such as Abu Ghraib, he emphasizes the system must allow the behaviors, even encourage them as many of the bylaws I encountered did, and it must include an authority figure, such as himself during the experiment.

In my case, the authority figure was played by the board chair. But it took him five years of dehumanizing me before he found a group willing to believe him. Once they believed that I was nothing more than an obstacle to be removed, their callous course was easy to follow.

Still, I too had to play an important role. Like those prisoners in the experiment I had to willingly dispose of myself and everything that made me an individual. The prisoners had their ambition of earning fifteen dollars a day. I jettisoned myself for my ambition of changing the world with bicycles through that job. Even after they fired me, it took me years to recognize the loss of my identity. I wrote the first draft of this book without including a shred of myself.

Now I know how easy it is to fall into the dehumanized role of victim (prisoner). But if the roles those young men played were determined only by the flip of a coin, that means that I, like anyone else, can just as easily fall into the role of the abuser. I scour my memory for times I may have done so. I remember the young man who was Thunderhead's executive director right before me.

As soon as I knew the job could be mine, I forgot him as if he was nothing, never asked if I could work with him on the transition and thus show respect for the work he had done.

I want this book to help others recognize when they fall into one of these roles and by recognizing it, find a way to escape. I'm sure that recognizing the abuse, as I did as a child, is primary. In Dr. Zimbardo's case, the intervention of his girlfriend was the only way he recognized it. I was so isolated during my job at Thunderhead and had deliberately shut my friends out, no one could alert me.

I have gained a deep appreciation for anyone who is stuck in an abusive relationship. I know now why my mother withstood my father's blows, her only action to take a knife to bed with her. I know now why my dog Jenny, just one month after I adopted her away from her abusive first home, cowered toward, not away from a man who kicked her. I know why those young men in that Stanford basement groveled instead of fled. Genocide has edged from beyond reason to explainable. There is an element of disbelief, certainty that it will end, that someone will stop them (or me, as that guard said). There may be a bit of complaining, but no concerted effort to stand up against the abuse, no campaign of the sort I've trained so many advocates to use to counter injustice. Instead there is a succumbing, a willing choice to go toward the abuse and let ourselves be wrapped into it. That disturbs and baffles me most. At least now I can empathize with those who are there.

I have learned that ambition is not to be trusted—that no single job is the only place to reach your dreams. I also now know that power is not something that anyone has. Power is something we give to others. The board chair lusted after power. I had the choice and chose to give it to him, just as the prisoners in the experiment enabled the power of the guards.

I read a sweet book recently about a dying man teaching a young man about life. It's called *Tuesdays with Morrie*, by Mitch Albom. Morrie tells Mitch that by learning how to die he is learning how to live, the theme of the book. It made me wonder whether by learning how to move beyond the bitter and resentful person I

This | 215

was immediately after Thunderhead, a sort of living death, I might be learning how to become a kind and perceptive person, like the gentleman outside the brew pub in Chicago who tried to warn me about the danger I was in. Perhaps I could be someone who stops to offer concern to a distraught stranger, who would never have to worry about becoming a "prisoner" or a "guard" again.

I keep reading, writing, noticing. I'm here with One Street and my pride in creating it, along with my bedrock of friends, ready to respond to what the world presents. But I'm haunted by what I experienced at Thunderhead. It pricks at me from the shadows, reminding me how blind I was during that time. In that self-doubt, I've lost the freedom I had as a hitchhiker. Back then I saw the whole world as my playground, like my reward for escaping abuse.

I stumbled upon a chance to reenter, feel, and be my former self several years ago, the last time I was in Uganda. I believe it was my first step back into myself, not just recognizing myself through my friends, but actually being myself. With that marker, I have steadily plodded forward and away from bitterness, feeling my way in the right direction because I felt it that day. There was nothing special about that day, no warning to prepare me for this time travel.

I'd spent the day with my eight women students guiding them first through chain repair and cleaning, then into rear hub disassembly, cleaning, greasing, and reassembly. They were a diverse group, their ages ranging from their twenties to our oldest in her seventies. Some were first and foremost mothers who fretted each day about their kids. Others were visionary entrepreneurs who asked pointed questions about opening their own bike shops in their villages. Most had never met each other before the course because each came from a different village, some walking hours in each direction.

But by that fourth day they were already close friends, their shoulders touching in tight circles as they scrubbed their parts, chatting and laughing over the buckets I'd set out for them in front of the workshop. We did most of our work out there because there wasn't much room inside for the whole group. We did, however, go in for the wheel truing and final bike assemblies using the professional tools and bike work stands that One Street had funded as part of the building of the new workshop.

On the day I had arrived, workers were still finishing the brick walls and the roof of the workshop so I was available to help them design the workbench and tool board, then place the bike work stands properly. We centered the workbench below the only window that looked out to a steep rainforested mountain that marked the border between Uganda and the Congo. On the opposite side of the small room, I helped the workers place hooks for hanging the rental bikes once the women had finished rebuilding them.

Working outside was my favorite. The workshop had an overhanging roof to cover a small deck and past that we had our class benches under a stand of shade trees. From there we could look full circle at the surrounding mountains covered in that dense primeval rainforest and hear the villagers passing by on the main village road on the other side of the hedgerow.

From the start, I had paired the students to ensure they would work through each day's lesson together. By the first day, I realized they would have helped each other anyway. Working with a translator, I gave them just enough information about that particular part to remove it from the bike and learn together how it functioned.

So that day, we'd had a lot of fun with those greasy snakes of chains as they splattered their colorful dresses and their hands smudged their bright head scarves. The shop aprons I'd provided couldn't cover all that vibrant cloth. I'd given up telling them to wear old clothes as they always arrived in long dresses and complementary scarves that seemed more suited for a fancy ball than a day wallowing in bike grease.

The rear hubs gave them plenty to puzzle over since they first had to remove the gears, each bike requiring its own unique tool. Every time one of them succeeded in pulling a set of gears free, the others would cheer and laugh before furrowing their brows again at their own stubborn wheels. Without my asking, those who had succeeded would join those still struggling to teach them what they'd learned about gear removal. By five o'clock, all chains were scrubbed bright and all rear wheels had been repacked with new grease and reassembled with spotless, freshly oiled gears. I congratulated them on another day they should be proud of and watched them walk together out the gate, their shoulders so much higher, so much more spring in their strides than that first timid day they'd arrived.

By then, I knew these capable women would never receive any support from the local organization that had persuaded me to raise the funds for the trip, the workshop, and the training. Still, watching them gain their confidence—whether through discovering their mechanical talents or by helping the others learn—I knew that each of these women would find a way to build on her abilities. Even without support to open their own bike shops, they could stand up against Uganda's inherent male chauvinism by fixing bikes men had given up on. They had everything they needed for their own Bike Hunts—to buy broken bikes and fix them for themselves, their families, or strangers in need of transportation. And I knew that at least a few of them would never let broken expectations stop them from opening their bike shops.

That evening was my turn to buy beer for the volunteers at the conservation camp where I was staying. Up the dirt road on the corner of the larger main dirt road through the village stood a bar. They called it the Good Shed Hotel, but it had no rooms to rent. I learned to question labels in Uganda. For instance, the "saloon" across the street from the "hotel" was a hair salon.

Along the ritual walk through the dark tunnel of trees up to the hotel to buy an armful of bottled beer, I replayed the events of the day—the women discovering then helping each other discover the traits of chains and hubs, all of it shadowed by my disappointment in that organization dropping its end of the project. Believing I had once again been blind, once again been fooled by someone else's false ambition as well as my own. Wondering if I would ever learn.

I stepped onto the covered walkway that wrapped the bar and

followed it past kids and other patrons to the entry, some of them greeting me by name. As I entered the open doorway into the candlelit room, the hostess greeted me and asked how many, no need to ask what I wanted. After a few weeks there, I was already a regular, which meant that the people talking loudly around the small tables and playing cards in the other room barely glanced up at me. So I leaned my back and elbows against the bar, propped a foot up, and let my disappointment disappear into that scene. But I drifted farther than I had expected. Without warning, I was back at any bar, any roadside diner, with everyday people finishing their day with a beer and some laughs. For that moment, before the hostess reappeared with the bottles, I let myself be back there in that time when only the moment mattered and all I had ahead of me was the next step.

Acknowledgements

Writing this book has been the hardest thing I've ever done. It would have remained a grim mirage had it not been for the caring and honesty of these exceptional people.

First I must thank the members of my writers' critique group in 2010—Joe Dibuduo, Lula Cooper, Bob Carlile, Karen Despain, Nancy Owen Nelson, and Irene Blinston—who showed me how horrible that first attempt was. Without their merciful bluntness I would have continued to force that bitter blather.

I credit my longtime river-guide friend, Jeffe Aronson, for inspiring me to give it another try, for shoving me off from shore once again. His own memoir efforts in late 2014 gave me the needed nudge to finally pull together all the disjointed notes and ramblings I'd stacked over the ensuing four years. Then, in early 2016 when I finally had a semblance of a book, he offered ideas for smoothing it out.

Elaine Jordan was my next reader and to my delight, found it readable. Her thoughtful suggestions helped me rearrange and prioritize elements of the early drafts.

My next readers still had their hands full. My dear tennis buddy, Dana Wingate, not only played an important role in my recovery, but conveyed his concern and clarity for revisions. Barbara Jacobsen, a fellow bike advocate, offered needed details and encouragement. Karen Nozik, my confidant and ally throughout the time of this story, helped me show the struggle better and reminded me of my admiration of bike advocates. James Moore, an invaluable supporter throughout, had sent a jolt of condolence and hope in a printed story and note that hangs on my office wall to this day. As an early reader, he also offered his important praise from his first-hand experience. Kathianne Crane, my sister-in-law, helped me wash away any lingering residue of bitterness and find the needed balance.

I owe special thanks to Thomas Cobb, author and mentor, for his stunning assertion that *Bike Hunt* is a love story.

Readers of the final draft took it on with care. Jim Knaup, my sweet husband who had endured the terrible journey with me, reminded me of my pride in overcoming its effects. Johanna Hawley, my partner in art and laughter, underscored the importance of telling this story. Michael Linke, my nonprofit and bike workshop colleague, highlighted points needing more emphasis as he empathized through his own experiences. John Hopkins, my bike advocacy colleague and a professional editor, combed through it to help me polish each intention and sentence to a fine sheen. And Lindsay Buroker, my tennis and writing buddy, provided technical help and advice.

My supporters during and after the time of this story were my beacons as my world was enveloped in darkness. To the brave Thunderhead members, partners, and board members who stood up for me over those five and a half years, I hope you understand how critical you were to my eventual recovery. To One Street's board members, advisors, and supporters, you gave me the firm foundation from which I was able to recover. And to my Swedish family and friends at and around the farm Hillsta, especially my brother Knut Hanner and my sister Heidi Karlsson, you never let me slip away.

Finally, I want to thank Jarek Slagowski, my boxing coach and friend, for being in my corner and for providing a place where I could fight through the reliving of this story.

Acknowledgements

www.ingramcontent.com/pod-product-compliance
Lightning Source LLC
Chambersburg PA
CBHW032054090426
42744CB00005B/204